I CAN'T WAIT TO BE PATIENT

(AND THE FASTEST WAY TO GET THERE)

DR. ROB BELL

Book Design: Fuel VM fuelvm.com
Published by: DRB Press

ISBN 978-1-7343588-3-4 (Hardback)
ISBN 978-1-7343588-4-1 (Paperback)
ISBN 978-1-7343588-5-8 (E-book)

ALSO BY DR. ROB BELL

Mental Toughness Training for Golf

The Hinge: The Importance of Mental Toughness

NO FEAR: A Simple Guide to Mental Toughness

Don't "Should" on Your Kids: Build Their Mental Toughness

50 Ways to Win: Pro Football's Hinge Moments

NO ONE Gets There ALONE

Puke & Rally: It's Not About the Setback, It's About The COMEBACK

Cantwaitbook.com

#CANTWAIT

 #CANTWAIT
@drrobbell

 #CANTWAIT
@drrobbell

Advanced Praise

"*Patience is a concept that's vital to high-performance and one that I am continuously trying to improve upon. This book provides great insight into ways that can be done.*"

— Rajeev Ram, Multiple Grand Slam Tennis Champion

"*Dr. Rob does an amazing job of breaking down the important elements of patience. I achieved my lifelong goal of a world champion the same year as undergoing my most severe injury. Patience and persistence!*"

— Felicia Stancil, Olympian/World Champion

"*Dr. Rob's book sheds light into the extreme power of patience. High-performers need to recover and patience is the recovery of the mind. As he states, 'If we can wait, then we can win.'*"

— Kevin Pritchard, President of Basketball Operations, Indiana Pacers

"*If you want to be healthy, happy, and successful in today's fast paced world you need to develop the skill of being patient with yourself and others. Dr. Rob's book is full of useful ideas for doing so.*"

— Dr. Bob Rotella, Sport Psychologist

"*Dr. Rob's 'I Can't Wait to be Patient' perfectly illustrates our constant need to focus on patience if we are to be successful. With the everyday pressures we all face, patience is the perfect foundational key to keeping grounded and focused.*"

— Adam Schenk, PGA Tour Player

"As a CEO, *I can't wait to be patient* is an incredible guide to how to think about time in our lives and maximize the different situations in our lives. It's a must read to dive deep into the perception of time and the fastest way to be patient."

— Jeff Byers CEO Momentous

"My favorite section of Dr. Rob's book is "this too shall pass." I resonate most with this because bad times don't come to stay. Staying Patient is hard, but rewarding!"

— Austin Cook, PGA Tour Winner

"*I Can't Wait To Be Patient* gives an insightful look into our relationship with our most precious commodity in life, our time. Dr. Rob Bell's ability to break down the mental skills required to become more urgent with our preparation yet be patient with our results is brilliant."

— Sandy Zimmerman, American Ninja Warrior

"Well done, Dr. Rob! Most successful people learn to embrace the "process." I Can't Wait To Be Patient provides ideas of how to maximize our process by combining the relentless pursuit of a goal with the patience to wait for the results."

— Joe Skovron, PGA Tour Caddy

"Prioritization is a major challenge for every businessperson, but Dr. Bell's book, I Can't Wait To Be Patient, does a great job of describing how urgency impacts our decision-making and how to overcome being overwhelmed."

— David Meltzer, Co-founder of Sports 1 Marketing

"Dr. Rob's book urges us to keep perspective and take advantage of the present moment in time. It reminds us that wins and losses are both guaranteed, and that there is an art in balancing urgency and patience."

— Katie Volynets, WTA professional, USTA National Champion

"Dr. Rob has hit a home-run with this book. In a world where we want tomorrow's results yesterday, he helps us understand and appreciate the path to success is through time. Written in Gladwellian manner, I highly recommend for performance based individuals."

— Nick Hardwick, Fitness Entrepreneur, Eleven-Year NFL Veteran

"Throughout my PGA Tour career, I've benefited from patience. Now, Dr. Rob has a book that can teach you, and in the fastest way possible."

— Scott Stallings, Multiple PGA Tour Champion

"Dr. Bell's introduction of the concept of "I can't wait to be patient" has changed the way I view not just my time, but my life."

— Casey Weade, Founder of Howard Bailey Financial

"If you are struggling with that breakthrough you've been working hard for, Dr. Rob Bell once again shows us the way. It's time for you to find the fastest way to get a copy of I Can't Wait To Be Patient!"

— Luke Tyburski, Ultra-Endurance Athlete & Keynote Speaker

"I couldn't wait for the book to come out, so wrote this blurb to get an advanced copy."

— John Brubaker, Impatient Author, Speaker & Executive Coach

"This is Dr. Rob's best book yet! We do indeed need to be urgent with the process and patient with the results."

— Tyler Duncan, PGA Tour Champion

Acknowledgements

To my family, Nicole, Ryan, and Porter.

One lifetime is all we have. But, if we do it right, one is enough. Let's keep crushing it together only towards that which is important.

Andrew Curtis, Kylie Hasenour and everyone at FuelVM.com

Thank you!

To Momentous, the best in-class.

Table of Contents

TRUSTED BY WORLD-CLASS EXPERTS AND RECORD-SETTING ATHLETES

Momentous has a deep portfolio of supplements and sports nutrition products designed to help you train harder, sleep better, and recover faster.

Visit Cantwaitbook.com

What's Your "Patience Personality?"

"The Fastest Way To Be Patient" Course

100 Miles

*"Life is not a sprint, but it's not a marathon either,
it's more like a 100-mile trail race."*

Process (noun): A series of actions, motions, or operations leading to some result.

Product (noun): A thing or person that is the result of an action or process.

In preparation for my 100-mile race with a thirty-hour cut-off, I ran over 1200 miles and upwards of 700 hours of training, stretching, traveling, recovering, and repeating the entire process.

There was a lot of preparation; I had sixteen different *training* runs close to a marathon distance of 26 miles. And I had an extremely difficult three-month stretch over the summer leading up to the race. It taught me a great lesson.

One of these difficult runs stood out. This particular trail run began at 5:30AM. Throughout the sunrise and the hot and humid August morning, I had about eight miles remaining of a twenty-six-mile run.

It sucked. As I batted away the horseflies, endured the inner thigh chafing, and soreness in my quads, I wanted the run to simply be over. I *couldn't wait* for the run to end.

And during these final miles, a transformational thought hit me. I realized that this difficult moment although relatively painful, held deep significance. I was in a fatigued state of realizing that there had to be meaning in the suffering. This suffering couldn't only be for the race itself.

The meaning from the suffering was simple to grasp, but not easy to apply.

I realized that I couldn't wish or hope for this run to end.

Time is hinged on a door that swings both ways.

Time possesses the same value and power regardless of any personal circumstances, opinions, or beliefs.

If I wished away the last eight miles on the trail, then I'd forfeit the gift of time, which was to be in the moment, right here and right now.

If I wished away the hurt of those final eight miles, then logically, wouldn't I have to wish away the celebrations as well? None of us get to choose to pause or slow down time during the good times and speed up time through the painful ones. If I *can't wait* for this run to be over, then I also *can't wait* for the good times to be over.

I never wanted the good times to end. My mindset always wanted the fleeting nature of the good times to last a little longer. In fact, my biggest struggles in life have come after the good times have ended.

But since the good times can't last, it also means the bad times can't last either.

This too shall pass...

Pain and pleasure are a package deal. We cannot choose one without the other. This was profound for me to grasp.

The lesson in that training run transferred into all areas of life because of the relationship with time. The preciousness of time became clearer. The amount of time dedicated to preparation helped reveal the utter importance of time.

All of us, no matter our field of expertise, spend more time preparing than actually performing. We practice more than we play.

And because of that lesson on the trail, *this too shall pass,* held true in the 100-mile race itself.

The race consisted of four twenty-five-mile trail loops. On the second loop, at mile forty-five, twelve hours into the run, I puked. It was a stressful period in the race.

I limped into the aid station at mile fifty with intestinal issues and still had fifty miles to run. The sun started to set and I planned for the rest stop to only take ten minutes to reset, change socks, get supplies, eat, and keep moving. However, I battled and literally watched the clock tick away for thirty minutes before starting off again. Those thirty minutes to me felt like ten minutes.

Often, when we encounter brutal, painful adversity, we distort time. Our perspective is off because we project into the future.

We think, *because I'm feeling this way right now, then I'll feel worse later.* This type of stinking thinking is based on the immediate reality, but with no patience towards the future.

During adverse situations, the reality is *"because I currently feel this way* ***does not*** *mean I'll feel worse later."* Just because the miles forty-five to fifty of our own race in life are awful does not mean that we will always feel this way.

This too shall pass...

Time possesses amazing power.

As I finished the 100-mile ultra-marathon, there was a range of emotions. There were, of course, feelings of joy, thankfulness, and success that I finished the grueling race. And I also got the customary belt buckle for the accomplishment.

These are mountain top moments.

We strive for a goal and finally reach the success we've been chasing after, hence the mountaintop. The mountaintop experience is unique. There is no one mountaintop moment that fits all. We think we know what success and accomplishment will feel like, but we can't until we experience it.

However, the mountaintop experience, no matter how wonderful the view, reaches a point in time. The time in which we must come back down off the mountain.

Our own mountaintop experiences were not permanent, just temporary. And this also shed light for me into the power of time.

This too shall pass extended into the mountaintop moment I experienced.

Days and weeks thereafter, my emotions and mood changed. I was left feeling sort of empty. Many Olympians and other ultra-runners have expressed similar feelings. There is such anticipation, planning, and preparation into the event, that there's somewhat of a comedown afterwards.

Think, after your own awesome accomplishment was over, was there a feeling of loss, disconnect, or a "what's next" mentality?

The experiences that accompanied the race itself were vast. However, as I got further away from the actual finish, the memories and transformation had more to do with the process rather than the product of the finish. And the process of training was more transformational than the product of the race itself.

Mountaintop moments are the result of the climb. The product. The finish.

The "product" is the result of the process. It's also how we see someone else's success and failure. Thus, there exists a tension between the process and product. Anyone not directly involved are only focused on results.

The product requires patience.

We want the product, the results, and the outcome. We want the mountaintop moment!

But, we all have a little bit of Veruca Salt in us. We want *it* and we want *it now...*

As wonderful as winning and success are, they are temporary. Success, accomplishment, and winning are fleeting. The product holds importance, but both good outcomes and bad outcomes are short-lived.

Since we all prepare way more than we perform, the process holds just as much importance as the product.

"The process" is a cliché. The process involves all the hours of preparation and practice — most of which is unseen by others. It contains the struggles, the losses, the setbacks, the meetings, the travel, the disagreements, isolation, injuries, arguments, sickness, family, and the managing of personalities.

The process takes perspective.

The reason why the process is so important is due to the relationship with time. Time provides us a gift, whether good or bad, *this too shall pass.* This shift in perspective merely demands an increased awareness, appreciation, and relationship of time.

The perspective is that we will receive the gift of our second wind. If we are patient with the situation and ourselves, we sometimes even receive our third, fourth, and fifth wind in life as well.

The product requires patience and patience brings forth perspective.

We can't wait to be patient.

However, if you can wait, then you can win.

The power of time

"We have two lives. And our second life starts after realizing there is only one."
— Confucius

Time has transformational power.

It is our most precious resource. We must first appreciate and understand our relationship with time in order to develop patience.

Since July 1st 1937, the Tomb of the Unknown Soldier at Arlington National Cemetery has been guarded for every second of every day. It has been the duty of The Honor Guard for The Tomb of The Unknown Soldier.

The Honor Guard duties are rigorous and it is a tremendous honor. The Tomb Guard Identification Badge is awarded to sentinels after a series of tests and nine months of guarding of the tomb. Because of the rigor, only 600 sentinels have been recognized with the award since the 1950's.

The Honor Guard marches in specific twenty-one step arrangements. Twenty-one symbolizes the 21-gun salute which is the highest honor bestowed in the United States military. They take precisely twenty-one steps and twenty-one seconds in-between movements at the end of each walk.

The changing of the guard is a sight to be witnessed. Each changing of the guard is so precise that perfection is the goal and each sentinel is graded after every change.

The heel strike and toe push are so exact for the guarding of the tomb, that one can witness the power of time. When you visit, your eyes are drawn to the indelible mark of footprints. The process of millions of steps in precision over time created a product of footprints.

The footprints of the Honor Guard at the Tomb of The Unknown Soldier are in stone.

Footprints in sand are natural. Footprints in stone however can only be accomplished through the transformational power of time.

For another example to help reveal the sheer power of time, one only needs to look at money.

Rich people have money, but wealthy people have time. Wealthy people use their money to actually have more available time.

The main principle behind wealth is patience.

Warren Buffet said it best when asked why everyone doesn't adopt his simple investment strategy. He said, *"because no one wants to get rich slow."*

If one started investing just $13 a day at the age of twenty-three, *assuming a return rate of 6%,* they will become a millionaire by the age of sixty-seven. If one started investing at age thirty-five, one would need to save $30 a day for the same return by age sixty-seven. And if someone waited until the age of forty-five, it would take *$63 per* day to reach millionaire status by age sixty-seven.

The miracle of "compounding" is a tool, which helps uncover the power of time. Compounding is the process of reinvesting one's earnings over time.

Wealth accumulates because one earns money on the principal invested and earnings from initial investment. Hence, compounding magnifies interest earned — over time.

Compounding is patience in action.

Warren Buffet's net worth at age thirty-six was approximately $8 million dollars. Not a bad nest egg, however, 8 million is not a reason why you know Warren Buffet's name.

With time, by age fifty-six, Warren Buffet's net worth was estimated at $1.4 billion. And by age sixty-six, his wealth had increased to 17 billion. By the age of ninety years old, his wealth had risen to approximately $93-100 billion dollars.

Here's another example of money that illustrates the strength of time.

If one invested $1000 in Apple stock (AAPL) in 1980, that investment would be worth 1.4 million, forty or so years later. And that does not include dividend payments or splits of the stock. However, if one invested $10,000 at the stock offering of AAPL, that money would have increased to $14 million dollars.

And one would not have had to be clairvoyant to experience the compounding effect of time on money. If one invested $1000 in the S&P 500 in the year of 1980, that investment today would be worth approximately $100,000.

Of course, the stock market is a tool that unleashed the positive influence of time. If one merely held onto the $1000 in 1980 and did nothing, inflation over time would reduce the buying power of $1000 to approximately just $250.

That is the transformational power of time.

Time grants money so much power that the stock market has never decreased in value. However, if you watched or listened to any financial shows, you'd be very hard pressed to find any evidence supporting that claim. Within the world of setbacks, monetary losses become instantaneous and excellent television fodder.

Now, of course, there have been short-term losses and setbacks within the stock market. Nonetheless, with time, the stock market has never lost money! The long-term reveals the power and influence of time and patience.

The global gross domestic product (GDP) is a great indicator of a country's economic health. In 2000, the global gross domestic product was approximately 33 trillion dollars. In the United States alone, circa 2000, the GDP was 10 trillion dollars.

To illustrate the power of time on wealth, in twenty-three years, the global GDP had risen to 84 trillion dollars and the United States GDP was 21 trillion dollars. That's an increase of 51 trillion dollars globally and 11 trillion dollars within the United States GDP.

The S&P 500 follows the largest 500 companies in the United States. Similar to the GDP, it provides another indicator of an economy's health. In the year 2000, the S&P 500 had an average closing price of $1427.22.

Twenty-three years of time later, the average closing price of the S&P index was over $4425. That's an average increase of the S&P 500 of almost $3000.

According to these examples, time is indeed money.

The harsh reality is that we do not value time the same as money. I agree with Zig Ziglar when he once stated, *"Money is important, second to oxygen."* Money is king.

However, if money is king, then time is queen. In the game of chess, effectively utilizing the queen is how the game is won.

If you feel that money is more important than time, then do you check the time or your bank account more often? For that matter, do you check your calendar or your checking account more frequently?

You have probably heard this analogy before, but imagine if every day, you were gifted with $84,600. How would you invest or spend your time?

The $84,600 question can resonate because we do possess 84,600 seconds every day. It's the relationship with time that matters.

— — —

Time is powerful.

Think of the importance of timing in life. It takes one moment, encounter, or meeting with someone to change the trajectory of lives. Timing is about being in the right place at the right time and taking full advantage of opportunities.

Time is universal and the only non-renewable resource that is the same for everyone. We can earn more money, make new friendships, opportunities, or experiences, whereas no one can create any more time.

Regardless of the many changes that take place in society and how we operate and whatever technological advances we use, time remains a constant.

Time is even personified. "Father time" is represented in classic paintings and sculptures. At every New Year, time is seen as an old man leaving and a newborn arriving.

Just think of the number of sayings of "time."

We save time.

We have time management.

We spend time.

We waste time.

We kill time.

We get lost in time.

We don't *have* time.

Only time will tell.

Time marches on.

Pressed for time.

The test of time.

It's a matter of time.

Time flies or time stands still.

Going through a tough time.

Time, after time, after time.

However…as clever as these pithy cliché's are, famed musician and writer Henry Rollins puts it differently, *"there is no such thing as spare time, no such thing as free time, no such thing as down time, all you got is life time."*

— — —

Where we encounter resistance with time is that we as a species are hardwired for speed, not patience.

We are designed to get from point A to point B as quickly as possible.

To illustrate, which program would you buy?

- *How to be rich in 90 days or less?*

Or

- *How to be rich in 7-9 years?*

Which of these is more appealing?

- *How to publish your book in 30 days or less?*

Or

- *How to publish your book in a year?*

These examples illustrate the appeal that speed has in our lives.

We assume speed and quickness equates to an easier path. We look at the examples above and automatically think of the time rather than the product it produces. Who wouldn't want a faster way?

Alas, we do not hop in our car, plug in the navigation, and pick the slowest or longest path. Life is the same way; we are built to start our journey and reach the mountaintop of results as efficiently as possible. We value quickness!

The importance we place on speed is also how we value time. And our hardwiring itself suggests that the speed of time is the most valuable resource. Society relishes and romanticizes ultra-high-speed and quickness.

Tools such as "Insta," "mobile ordering," "5G or 6G or 7G internet speed," "binge watching," "same-day delivery," "artificial intelligence," and "live betting" have all made such activities in life faster and seemingly more convenient. There is also the speed from artificial intelligence, predicative analysis, and big data. Big data has become big business.

These examples merely reveal the massive increase of speed in society as a whole. Technology has quickened and even changed the rhythm of life. And as a result of increased tempo and cadence of life, our patience has decreased. Why must we have patience when the answers, goods, and services are immediately available?

Nonetheless, even with our love of speed, society also appears to uphold patience as a virtue.

It stresses restraint, being tolerant of others, focusing on the process, paying your dues, and a step-by-step approach toward betterment. Ironically, even though we are built to get from point A to point B as efficiently and effortlessly as possible, we under-value our relationship with time.

Time itself has even dominated the scoreboard for excuses.

The all-time number one excuse has been, *"I don't have the time"* or "I'm too busy." Time has been used so frequently and accepted by others that no other excuse is even a close second.

Of course, what we are actually saying is *"I don't have control over my time."* Or *"I don't want to tell you no"* or *"I don't have [it] as a real priority."*

Our mental wellness has suffered due to our strained relationship with time. We are bombarded by the urgent, tugged by the future, and distracted and discouraged by the unimportant.

Burned out, overwhelmed, worried, rushed, tired, and too busy are descriptors with which we all can relate. "Life" is complex with kids, travel, bank accounts, appointments, and activities. Society as a whole has reported that we are more rushed, hurried, anxious, and pressed for time than during any other period.

It has been reported as a "time famine" because there is simply too much to do. Many think time is a thief and a thief that can't be caught. We look at it as a villain in our lives and blame it mercilessly when we aren't "there" fast enough.

The irony is that we have more available 'time' to us now than at any point in history. We possess more *leisure time* than ever before. However, because we are programmed for quickness, our leisure time has even sped up.

Time is undefeated. But many think of time as an opponent. It must become an ally, not an opponent, in order to win the challenges we face. The product takes patience, and no matter how much we adore speed and quickness, we can't fast forward the process.

Patience is the path.

When we improve our relationship with time, our attitude and outlook will change for the better as well.

Birth of Kevlar

Stephanie Kwolek finished college in 1946 and her lifelong work as a chemist began. She specialized in creating a material as hard as steel, but lighter. Ten years passed throughout the many experiments and her fellow chemists had given up on the idea. At last, a serendipitous find helped her create the first group of synthetic fibers known as Kevlar. *Patience* has literally saved thousands of lives.

Time is relative

"Today is the oldest you've ever been and the youngest that you'll ever be."
— Eleanor Roosevelt

One of Albert Einstein's discoveries was the theory of relativity. Einstein determined that the rate in which time passes is relative to our own frame of reference.

Three minutes of an ice-bath and three minutes of conversation are interpreted, processed, and perceived differently. Three minutes of running sprints is a different feeling and experience than three minutes of a casual walk. Three minutes of intense focus on a problem is a different experience than three minutes of watching television and so on.

Time is relative to our frame of reference.

For a child in the third grade, their entire life to that point is literally spent in the third grade. The school year seems like it is an eternity and the summer itself rushes by. How many times have we heard *"The summer went too fast"* when returning for a new school year?

The school year seems like an eternity to a third grader because of their point of reference. The middle childhood years of development are massive. An 8-year-old, one school year is an eternity.

Think of time as a percentage of life.

We have our actual time of existence, and we have our overall percentage of experience. One full year for an 8-year-old makes up almost 90% of their life experiences to date! However, one full year for an 80-year-old is only 5% of their entire life experience.

The teenage years in particular are ones that contain much acclaim and milestones such as turning sixteen and eighteen years of age. These years can sometimes feel long as well, in anticipation of *I can't wait to turn eighteen…*

One year for a 15-year-old is approximately 80% of their life. Thus, it's no wonder that they know it all at that age.

Juxtaposed to a 50-year-old, one year of existence now merely makes up 40% of their entire experience. They've seen the seasons, the changes, the good and bad, and with a snap of the fingers, it's gone.

Here's an illustration of how the relativity of time is represented by a percentage of life.

Years of life represents = a percentage of total life experience.

1 year of life represents

- 8-year-old existence = 90% of total life experience
- 10-year-old existence = 87.5% of life experience
- 15-year-old existence = 81.3% of life experience
- 18-year-old existence = 77.5% of life experience
- 21-year-old existence = 73.8% of life experience
- 25-year-old existence = 68.8% of life experience
- 30-year-old existence = 62.5% of life experience
- 35-year-old existence = 56.3 % of life experience
- 40-year-old existence = 50% of life experience
- 45-year-old existence = 43.8% of life experience
- 50-year-old existence = 37.5% of life experience
- 55-year-old existence = 31.3% of life experience
- 60-year-old existence = 25% of like experience
- 65-year-old existence = 18.8% of life experience
- 70-year-old existence = 12.5% of life experience
- 75-year-old existence = 6.3% of life experience

We can look at life in specific days as well. Based on a lifetime of eighty years of life, there are 29,220 days. Depending on our age, there are a certain number of days *remaining.*

- 8-year-old = 2,922 days alive = 26,298 days remaining
- 10-year- old = 3,652 days alive = 25,568 days remaining
- 15-year-old = 5,479 days alive = 23,741 days remaining
- 18-year-old = 6,575 days alive = 22,645 days remaining
- 21-year-old = 7,670 days alive = 21,550 days remaining
- 25-year-old = 9,131 days alive = 20,089 days remaining
- 30-year-old = 10,957 days alive = 18,263 days remaining
- 35-year-old = 12,783 days alive = 16,437 days remaining
- 40-year-old = 14,610 days alive = 14,610 days remaining
- 45-year-old = 16,436 days alive = 12,784 days remaining
- 50-year-old = 18,262 days alive = 10,958 days remaining
- 55-year-old = 20,088 days alive = 9132 days remaining
- 60-year-old = 21,915 days alive = 7305 days remaining
- 65-year-old = 23,741 days alive = 5479 days remaining
- 70-year-old = 25,567 days alive = 3653 days remaining
- 75-year-old = 27,394 days alive = 1826 days remaining

This chart, like all speculation, is not incorrect. It is just incomplete.

You may live longer than eighty years or you may live shorter than the speculated 29,220 days.

Time is relative.

The last few days of a vacation seem to move faster than the first few days. At the start of a vacation, everything is new and in anticipation. But, as the vacation progresses, the closer we get to the end of a trip, anticipation has been replaced with memories and experiences instead.

In competition contexts, the anticipation of the event can possess an anxious feeling. We *can't wait* for the moment to play and compete. In weekly life, Friday has a feel and anticipation of the upcoming evening and weekend. Sunday evenings have a certain feel and may have us in a different mood as well.

Life is quite similar with perception of time.

When we're young, we don't think about time. Everything and every experience are new or at least newer. However, the older we get, time now becomes a major focus. There are fewer new things and there is more routine instead.

In one regard, the 2020 pandemic seemed like such a long time ago, but the effects can sometimes still be witnessed, and we are reminded how recent it was.

Father of Modern South Africa

Nelson Mandela was sent to prison in 1964. He spent twenty-seven years as a political prisoner and was released in 1990. He brought an end to Apartheid and fostered a new peace in South Africa. He became the first president of South Africa in 1994, proclaimed a new constitution, and received the Noble Peace Prize.

A clock with no hands

"Time is what we want most, but what we use worst."
— William Penn

Supply and demand is a cornerstone of economic theory. Prices increase with less supply, coupled with more demand.

Time fits within the supply and demand paradigm. When we are young or younger, we have unlimited supply of time and little demand. Hence, the price or value we place on it is inexpensive. The older we get, however, the less supply of time that we have, and the time demands increase. Hence, as we age, we place a much higher value on time.

The supply and demand with time is why procrastination affects the age group of 14/29-year-olds the most. It's difficult to appreciate time when younger because there's such an abundance. Research has shown that we outgrow procrastination because our relationship with time. Our appreciation of time coupled with the scarcity of time results in reduced procrastination. [1]

The clock and days alive are just an approximation. Hence, we live with a clock with no hands.

We live under the illusion that we are in control of when we live or die. Over 6,000 people die every hour. For most, this illusion is real to us like a rainbow.

But, life and death can extend to other areas. This could mean when a relationship ends, a career shift, or when our playing days are over. It could relate to when a major loss occurs or an injury happens.

We do not know when or what will be our final moment in a variety of life circumstances.

A clock with no hands means that no one can predict when natural disasters, famines, heart attacks, housing crises, or a pandemic will emerge. No one knows when his/her last moment or final experience of something will take place. The pandemic erased a season for many athletes who graduated and never got another chance to play. They didn't know it would have been their last.

A personal example, our daughter used to hold her mommies earlobes while watching T.V. Our daughter laid in her lap and would reach up and hold on until the ear became too hot. It was one of those cute memories. And then, one day, she no longer did it. It was over.

What is accurate about living on a clock with no hands is that there will be highs and lows. There will be wins and losses, celebrations and adversity. Both of these are guaranteed.

And setbacks and struggle will occur more often than any of us would like to admit. We just don't know when or how they will transpire.

On the positive slant, a *clock with no hands* also means we must relish the mountaintop moments of achievement, celebration, and peace. Another mountaintop is not guaranteed.

A clock that grows legs

"If youth only knew and if old age only could."
— Henri Estienne

Many think health is our greatest resource. When we are healthy, time is to our advantage. We can choose to spend it however we want. However, when our health is taken away, or if we live in chronic pain, our time can become limited.

Dave Meltzer described it succinctly, *"When you're healthy, you have thousand of wishes everyday. However, when you're unhealthy, you have one wish."*

When we are sick, injured, and suffering, however, time can become the greatest healer. Even if the health diagnosis is terminal, the clock can give us new perspective and appreciation for everything we take for granted.

A clock with no hands represents not really knowing where we are with life's moments.

However, when the clock grows legs, there is now a premium placed on time. And when we focus on time, we realize how precious it is. When someone receives a terminal diagnosis for instance, the clock grows legs, and every moment alive is better appreciated.

Only with experience can we realize the most precious resource is time. Time spent with loved ones, time doing the things we want to do, time pursuing greatness, and time simply spent living.

It's as we get older that we see that the clock grows legs. A countdown towards an accomplishment, goal, or end date has begun for example.

Certain events can make us hyper-aware of the speed of time. The simplest and most common examples in our life are when we enter and exit high school; the clock grows legs in terms of our grade level and graduation within four years. Each school year becomes more significant as well. Hence, a sense of urgency enters the fray, as the finish line gets closer. When we finish, only then can we see how fast it all went.

The same clock resets again as we enter college. A sense of urgency can become more amplified as we easily stare into the future and what it holds after graduation. Before we know it, we are done.

The clock seems to grow massive, strong legs when children are born. There's a time stamp, a specific point of reference with our lives, and we begin counting up.

As our kids start to age, we measure our own lifetime based upon the precise chronology of our kid's lives. Their birth or their youth or graduation seemed almost like yesterday, yet at the same time, it seemed like a lifetime ago. The days are long, but the years are fast!

The Longest-Winning Streak In Sport

The America's Cup was first competed in 1851. The New York Yacht Club (NYYC) would hold the prestigious sailing cup for over 132 years. It was quite simply the longest streak in sports. At one point, human hands did not touch the trophy itself in over 100 years. However, in 1983, the Royal Perth Yacht Club represented *The Australia II*, skippered by John Bertrand, and finally won.

I can't wait

"It's how we behave while waiting."
— Joyce Meyer

"I can't wait" is a wonderful euphemism. It signals excitement and anticipation of an event.

For example, we utter, "I can't wait to play" or "I can't wait to start" or "I can't wait until springtime" or "I can't wait for that movie."

However, it is boldly inaccurate. Whatever the anticipation of an event, we will wait.

We can wait and frankly, we have to wait. There is no other option.

For some, waiting can even be a traumatic event. If you've ever been stranded at an airport overnight, then you can relate. A study revealed "shocking" results of participants having to "wait." They could wait alone for 15 minutes or shock themselves, and 67% of men chose to shock themselves instead of being alone with their thoughts. [2]

It's how we behave while waiting.

Standing in a slow line, uncertain and worried about the wait can make waiting seem much longer. The uncertain waiting on a phone for customer service can itself cause anxiety and stress. There's a reason within television why a clock displays to us how long until the show is resumed.

Yet, we will still wait.

- We will wait an average of five years of our entire life just waiting in lines.
- The average individual will spend approximately thirty-eight hours each year in traffic.
- The average wait time to see a physician is twenty-six days.
- We spend approximately two years of our lifetime just in the bathroom.
- We sleep for almost twenty-six years of our lives and seven years is spent trying to *get* to sleep. [3]

Life and situations force us to wait. There will be curveballs and setbacks. We will have events that are unresolved and thus deal, handle, and cope with inconveniences, adversity, and sometimes tragedies.

- Anyone who has experienced an injury or broken bone has been forced to wait.
- The healing of ending close relationships requires time.
- It takes time to recover from a loss or getting fired.
- Growing a garden or baking a cake requires patience.
- Parenting…
- Success and greatness in any field demands the utmost of patience.
- Have you ever drunk wine before it's ready?

During the post-pandemic return to normalcy, a new moniker, *The Great Wait*, emerged. It was a state of limbo that represented *"a certainty that uncertainty will continue."*

We can't make water in a pot boil any faster no matter how hungry we are or how intently we watch it. But, just like our goals and purpose, it's important to know what we are cooking. Sometimes it's better to simmer to boil rather than to boil water as fast as possible.

Patience is hard!

We think we can't wait, but we will have to wait.

However, if you can wait, then you can win.

Sorry, but there are no five-step plans to nirvana, no one can write a great book for you under X number of days, and earning a million dollars *fast* doesn't exist.

Hacks, promises of overnight success, fads, and quick fixes all exist to sell you on the idea of speed. People pay for these ideas and hacks, however, because everyone wants to get from point A to point B in his or her journey as fast as possible.

And even though we can consume information and entertainment and goods very quickly, we can't fast forward success. No matter what, the product takes patience.

However, since none of us enjoy waiting, or are good at waiting, we try to avoid waiting by taking action.

But, you'll see that action, while important, is not always the best way to wait.

First Win on LPGA Tour

Ryann O'Toole became a professional golfer in 2010. She didn't win her first LPGA event until 2021 at the Scottish Open. It was her 228th start. Just prior to the win, she had contemplated retiring from the game.

Our Action Bias

"Have patience with all things but first of all with yourself."
—Francis De Sales

We have an extreme bias toward action.

Action bias *is where people favor action over inaction; even where there is no indication that doing so leads to a better result.*

Action is an impulse so strong that it leads the charge with the attitude of *"don't just sit there, do something."*

We perceive action as beneficial to inaction because it provides a sense of control and feeling of superiority over the potential outcome.

However, as you'll witness, action is not always better and can even lead to a worse result.

When the doctor is away, the mice will play

"The hurrier I go, the behinder I get."
— Anonymous

Cardiac arrest is one of the top medical emergencies and it is even deemed a public health crisis.

When one's heart suddenly stops beating, nine out of ten people die from cardiac arrest if outside of a hospital. If one is fortunate enough to arrive at a hospital in time, the survival rate increases to approximately 50%.

Myocardial infarction or a heart attack entails the stoppage of blood flow to the heart. It is sometimes a precursor to cardiac arrest. If a heart attack is a plumbing problem, then cardiac arrest is an electrical problem.

Unfortunately, many people ignore the warning signs of a heart attack, since the symptoms can be masked as chest pain or shortness of breath. A heart attack occurs in the United States approximately every forty seconds and it kills over one million people annually in the United States.

Life and death situations are indeed both important and urgent concerns. They are called *emergency rooms* and *urgent care* for a reason.

One would logically hope that the top doctors be available if a loved one were admitted to the hospital for such a high-risk situation.

However, is it possible that research suggests otherwise?

Interestingly, researchers examined death rates of heart attack hospitalizations between the years of 2002-2011 when the top doctors attended national conferences. [4]

The researchers examined the mortality rates of patients who were admitted to the emergency room with a heart attack. They observed patients for thirty-days after admission.

The results were contrary to our assumptions of top health care.

The mortality rate of high-risk patients was 17% when the doctors were away at a national conference, compared to 24.8% of deaths that occurred with the non-conference dates. [4]

Patients admitted to the hospital were *more likely* to survive a heart attack during cardiology national conference dates.

The authors of the study offered the "less is more" approach to help explain decreased mortality rates. Doing "nothing" resulted in more lives being saved than performing surgery.

The on-call cardiologists were reluctant to perform interventions based on a risk-benefit tradeoff. The potential harms of invasive interventions and procedures simply outweighed the benefits.

There was a reduction in specific procedures within the hospitals for these high-risk patients.

Researchers discovered that one of the main barriers for physicians was uncertainty and disagreement about what "not" to do. There exist specific guidelines and routines at the national, regional, and local level of care, which often sadly contradict one another. [5]

At risk of potential harm of invasive treatment, cardiologists on-call sided with avoiding surgery. And it resulted in more lives being saved.

When the cat's away, the mice will play. However, in this case, the mice were playing nice.

Five notable physicians' strikes have occurred between the years of 1976 and 2003. These strikes lasted between nine days and seventeen weeks. [6]

Medical doctors do not frequently participate in strikes. There are ethical concerns and criticism due to strikes adversely affecting patients' health. So, when they occur, just like other essential service industries, panic and fear can result.

However, in every case of physicians' strikes, the mortality rate stayed the same or decreased, but it never increased.

For instance, during 1976, doctors in Columbia went on strike for fifty-two days, and mortality rates dropped by 35% during that time.

When doctors in Los Angeles went on strike over working conditions and wages, mortality rate dropped 18%.

In 2000, Israeli doctors went on strike. The strike resulted in hundreds of thousands of outpatient visits being canceled along with thousands of elective procedures. [7]

The Jerusalem Post surveyed the non-profit burial society, which performs over 55% of burial services in Jerusalem. During the strike, the number of funerals performed in the region dropped significantly compared to data from the previous three years.

These results align with the studies of top cardiologists attending conferences. Even in health care, there exists an action bias and an inability to wait.

Researchers have even cited that "Physicians are wrong when they tell terminally ill patients 'doing something' (in other words, pursuing treatment) is better than doing nothing" ("nothing" usually meaning choosing hospice care instead of treatment). [8]

Clinical uncertainty is a balancing act. Doctors have reported a need to do something in order to soothe the emotions of patients. For instance, the global medical community has prompted initiatives to reduce the number of antibiotics prescribed. Nonetheless, research has repeatedly shown that clinicians prefer to *"err on the side of caution"* and provide the patient antibiotics *just to be safe*. [9]

Ordering a test, intervention, or medicine is a way of doing something rather than nothing and waiting. This action supposedly assures patients that everything will be all right. Doing something occurs way more often than waiting and re-evaluating the symptoms.

However, perhaps, if we can wait, then we can live.

I can't wait... to call timeout

"In theory, theory and reality are the same,
but in reality, they are different."
— Benjamin Brewster

"*Double Doink.*" Sometimes when the situation fits, words encapsulate an entire sports play. Chicago Bears fans remember the kick.

In a 2018 NFC playoff game vs. the Philadelphia Eagles at Soldier Field, the game was 16-15 in favor of the Eagles. As time was running out, Cody Parkey for the Chicago Bears set up for a game-winning 43-yard kick. The ball was snapped and kicked, just as the Eagles called time-out.

Icing the kicker is a term that represents a head coach calling time-out, which is intended to make the kicker miss the attempt. The thought process and belief is that the kicker's performance will decline in such situations due to the added perceived pressure.

Head coaches call time-out to allow more time for the kicker to *"think and process,"* which is intended to interrupt the rhythm, flow, and execution of a kicker's routine.

The Eagles timeout nullified the play, and both teams lined up again for the attempted field goal. This time, however, the ball hit the left upright and then struck the crossbar before eventually falling into the end zone and missing.

The words of the missed kick would come to be signified as the *"double doink."*

There are a number of studies examining the validity of calling time-out on the outcome of field goals.

The most robust research stems from Clark et al., in 2013 titled *"Going for three: predicting the likelihood of field goal success with logistical regression."* [10]

They specifically examined the *final ten seconds of a game* when NFL coaches called time-out to "ice the kicker." The researchers examined data of game winning or losing field-goal attempts from twelve consecutive seasons, 2000-2011.

Contrary to popular opinion, calling time-out and "icing the kicker" is not statistically significant, meaning it does not work beyond normal distribution of field goal attempts. And some analytics revealed that calling time-out might even work to the kicker's favor.

Instead of coaches calling *time-out*, research has shown environmental factors played a significant role in the successful attempts of a field goal. Distance of the kick is the greatest variable of course, but temperature, field surface, wind, precipitation, and altitude have all been shown to be statistically significant detriments with field goal percentage. Specifically, cold temperatures, wind, and precipitation reduced the likelihood of a successful kick.

In fact, when poor weather conditions are at play, calling time-out actually favors the kicker. The time-out in poor weather provides the kicker additional preparation time for all of the mentioned factors.

Yet, despite "icing the kicker" not working beyond randomness, head coaches still call time-out.

These coaches have spent their entire lives inside of the game and are paid to know more than anyone else, including the sports media. They are aware of the statistics, yet many still act upon the heuristic of "icing the kicker."

It's the action bias. Even the best coaches, at the highest level, often want to feel like, *"I'm doing something to influence the game."*

There's also a long-held ritual of not taking time-outs into the locker-room with you. Just because a head coach has a time-out remaining at the end of a game essentially means they feel additional pressure to use it.

And they do…

And perhaps more importantly, it is the perception of an action bias that makes an impact on their decision-making. The first question from sports media after a coach does not call time-out would be: *"Why didn't they call a timeout"?*

The opposite is rarely true; coaches would not be asked, *"Why did they call a timeout?"*

What exists more than statistical evidence is anecdotal evidence of a missed field goal kick. Anyone can look at an example where a coach called time-out and the kicker subsequently missed the kick, hence, *"double doink."*

There are tons of descriptors for big misses more so than successful kicks. When misses happen, the kicker becomes the sole culprit for a loss. There are not many, if any, deciding field goal attempts that don't warrant the microscope of profound criticism if it's missed.

And kickers have been fired after such misses.

When a deciding field goal is successful, however, it is lauded, but the entire team is celebrated and praised beyond the kicker. In these situations the adage is true, *"success has a thousand fathers, but failure is an orphan."*

However, no matter what decision takes place on the field, NFL kickers will still miss field goals. And since the negative far outweighs the positive, it is often the misses that we remember way longer than a winning kick.

And yes, as a result of the *double doink*, the Chicago Bears released Cody Parkey in the off-season.

Action is the answer, what was the question?

"Patience is the art of concealing your patience."
— Guy Kawasaki

The short-term isn't incorrect, but it is incomplete. We overvalue the short-term and undervalue the long-term.

We incorrectly view the short-term through a microscope and the long-term through a telescope.

The short-term is over-scrutinized and over-analyzed. The issue is that the short-term is simply a snapshot, not an entire movie. It is filled with emotion. It's about today's trend, today's headlines, today's statistics, and today's win/loss record. However, it's even more scrutinized than that, because it's about this exact moment, our feelings right now, or our immediate mood.

Issues arise when we only focus on the short-term. We immediately extrapolate it into the long-term. We think and act that just because the short-term is good or bad, then it will continue that way. We speculate and fast-forward through all of the positive and negative scenarios and outcomes.

The short-term focus isn't incorrect, but it is incomplete. For example, Hall of Fame professional football coaches Bill Walsh, Tom Landry, and Jimmy Johnson started off their collective careers with a win/loss record of 0-25.

Never forget, the results or product is a long-term campaign. One ingredient called for within the recipe of success always includes short-term sacrifice for long-term achievement. Patience and over-valuing the long-term means going beyond time management hacks and tactics.

We need to know *when* to be urgent and *how* to be patient.

However, waiting in the short-term may cause us to feel discomfort, unease, or uncertainty. And we act since we don't like that feeling of waiting.

Waiting in the short-term causes us to act.

— — —

I rarely come across any self-help posts that don't tout motivation, discipline, habits, and the simple fact that *"you must do the work."*

Action is wholeheartedly needed. Action does change everything. We all intuitively know that we can't just read the directions and expect a cake to appear.

Unfortunately, there are those people in life who wait for just the perfect moment to get started. They continually are "getting ready to get ready." Waiting for that perfect moment, but that day never comes. And unfortunately, no action ever gets taken. Or some steps are taken, but then abandoned. That's not you.

The most significant figures in life have taken action. In every story of change, innovation, and progress, action was taken.

Rock N' Roll Hall of Famer Diana Ross stated, *"You can't just sit there and wait for people to give you that golden dream. You've got to get out there and have to make it happen for yourself."*

One of the greatest athletes of all-time, Wayne Gretzky, commented about action, *"You miss 100% of the shots you don't take."*

One of the most influential and pious individuals of the 20th century, Mahatma Gandhi, also favored action. One of my favorite quotes, he stated, *"You may never know what results come of your actions, but if you do nothing, there will be no results."*

Physics even backs the conception of action. Sir Isaac Newton's first law of motion is *"an object at rest stays at rest and an object in motion stays in motion."*

Research studies have even shown that regardless of outcome, we evaluate action as more positive than inaction. Inaction is viewed with more negative outcomes.

Researchers presented two hypothetical soccer coaches, soccer Coach A and soccer Coach B, who both lost previous games by scores of 0-4. Coach A decided to take *action* and substitute three different players for the next game. Coach B took *inaction* and decided not to substitute any players. Both teams lost the next game 0-3.

Even though the losses were identical for both games, coaches that *did not* take action with the line-up were viewed more unfavorably and with possessing more regret. [11]

We are wired to act, move, solve problems, communicate, build relationships, and to get better.

It isn't a matter of "if" we should act; the questions we continually need to address is "when" and "how" to act?

We need to know *when* to act, and *how* to be patient.

As the professional examples revealed, we have an action bias. There's such an impulse toward action that it is our default answer. Action dominates the answer so much that the question matters less.

How do we respond when our emotions tell us to hurry, fix this situation, or watch out?

The impulse and belief is that **something** has to be better than doing **nothing**.

The bias *"don't just sit there, do something"* appears way better than the alternative, which is *"don't just do something, sit there"* mentality.

When we are driving along in life and hit a boulevard of green lights, by all means, keep doing what you're doing, staying aggressive, crushing it, and "making hay." Keep the actions going…

However…

When we are uncertain, consumed with adversity, filled with doubt, frustration, or loss, is still doing **anything** better than doing **nothing**?

Unfortunately, too often our action is miss-directed only towards that which is urgent in the moment.

There are situations, however, where action merges with the urgent and the important.

These are called emergencies.

---

504 Sit-In

Judy Heumann and Kitty Cone were both disability rights activists. They helped organize a sit-in at the federal building at 50 United Nations Plaza in San Francisco. The sit-in was orchestrated to protest the failure to enact section 504 of the Rehabilitation Act. On April 5th, 1977 approximately 150 Americans with disabilities and allies occupied the federal building. They refused to leave until Joseph Califano, secretary of health, education, and welfare signed the regulations that affected the disability population. On April 28th, 1977, he signed the regulation. It still is the longest sit-in to date inside of a federal building. The sit-in was of historic importance and ultimately led to the Americans with Disabilities Act.

Emergencies = urgency toward the important

"While we have time, let us do good."
— St. Francis of Assisi

Urgency is defined as requiring swift action. It means acting with clarity and purpose.

Urgency is execution of the important. Urgency is a state of the internal, not a state of the external. As Hall of Fame Coach Wooden often stated, *"Be quick, but don't hurry. I want quickness under control."*

Orio Palmer was deputy chief of Battalion 7 of the New York Fire Department. He was amongst the first to arrive on the scene at the World Trade Center during the 9/11 attacks.

The south tower of the World Trade Center was struck between the 77th and 85th floors at 9:03 am. Orio Palmer knew, as did all of the first responders present, that there were hundreds of people above the impact zone that needed to be rescued.

Orio Palmer single-handedly repaired an elevator in the South Tower and took it to the 40th floor. He then ascended on foot up the stairwells to the impact zone. Wearing full firefighter gear of about 50-60 pounds, he ascended to the 78th floor in minutes.

It was around the 78th floor that he found the only stairwell intact. He was able to reach survivors on the impacted floors. It was described that Orio Palmer was *"ensuring calm in the stairwells, assisting the injured and guiding the evacuees on the lower floors."*[12]

Tragically, just a few minutes after the last transcribed communication from Orio Palmer at 9:59am, the south tower collapsed.

Historian Peter Charles Hoffer described the audio transcripts as such: *"Listening to Palmer and his comrades on the recovered tape, one can hear the urgency of men working at high efficiency, but there was never a hint that the clock was running out on them."*

Welles Crowther was a civilian inside of the south tower on that fateful day. His office was on the 104th floor and was above the impact zone as the plane cut through the building. Welles carried an individual on his back approximately seventeen floors down and escorted a group of individuals down the south stairwell.

He also traversed back up to the 78th floor and another survivor, Judy Wein, who had a broken arm and broken ribs, watched as he helped administer first aid and extinguish the fire. She said that Welles announced to the entire floor, *"Everyone who can stand, stand now. If you can help others, do so."*[13]

Judy Wein also remarked that it was the demeanor in how he spoke that commanded action and saved souls. Welles Crowther helped save eighteen lives that day inside of the tower.

These two heroes, Orio Palmer & Welles Crowther, were in the same area before the tower collapsed.

Welles Crowther was twenty-four years old at his death. He was a volunteer firefighter and had played college lacrosse at Boston College. Welles's story can be observed in the documentary, *Man in Red Bandana*.

Orio Palmer was forty-five years old at the time of his death. He won the NYFD physical fitness award five times and was a marathon runner. Posthumously the FDNY's fitness award was renamed the Orio Palmer Memorial Fitness Award.

During this emergency, these two, amongst hundreds of others, acted with urgency. They acted with clarity of purpose and they behaved in a way that also inspired calm in others. There was not panic.

Although their stories had tragic endings, their legacy lives on. They effectively operated with urgency toward the important, quickness under control.

15 Seconds...

"Urgent trials awaken eager prayers."

E li Dicken, twenty-two, was at a mall with his girlfriend on a Sunday in July when they stopped at a pretzel stand in a food court. The time was 5:56 pm.

From thirty to forty yards away in the crowded food court, a man with an assault rifle and several magazines of ammunition exited the restroom. He started shooting innocent bystanders and fired a total of twenty-four rounds in just fifteen seconds.

From 2001-2021 there were 464 active shooter situations in the United States. In seventy-two cases, a bystander stopped the active shooter before police had arrived.

Eli Dicken increased the number to seventy-three cases.

From the distance of thirty yards, Eli steadied himself against a pole and fired ten rounds at the active shooter. The active shooter was shot dead as he attempted to retreat back to the restroom.

Sadly, three people were killed and two others were wounded, but a great number of lives were saved that day.

Fifteen seconds…it was fifteen seconds of murder before Eli Dicken responded and ended the threat for innocent people. Eli Dicken had no formal training within the police or military, yet he responded with bravery and clarity of purpose.

Emergencies represent urgency toward the important. These heroic examples within emergencies represent the truest form of urgency.

It is the blend of the important and the urgent. And emergencies are so undeniably important, that there often is little slack toward the unimportant or trivial issues.

These illustrations of heroes under duress represent urgency toward the important.

Inside of our own lives, urgency is a necessary ingredient for production and performance.

But, urgency by itself is a lunatic. If everything in life is urgent, then fast is the only speed we have toward everything. And urgency toward everything will cause stress, anxiety, and feeling overwhelmed.

It is imperative that we operate with important urgency. But, we first have to understand the influence of urgency.

Urgency trumps the important

*"I have two kinds of problems, the urgent and the important. The
urgent are not important, and the important are never urgent."*
— Dwight D. Eisenhower

Researchers wanted to examine the link between people's behavior for
tasks that were considered urgent compared to tasks that were
considered important. [14]

Participants were given a simple task to finish. It involved writing a quick
review for a product and it took one minute to complete.

The reviews were identical in difficulty, however they were weighed
differently. Task A was worth six points, whereas task B was worth ten
points. The participants would receive a prize for the more points that
they accumulated.

Thus, the research question: which task would the participants select? The
wrinkle that they introduced into the study was a sense of urgency.

Participants were told that task A *(6 points)* would only be available for
ten minutes, while task B *(10 points)* would be available for twenty-four
hours.

In the study, when a sense of urgency was introduced, it competed directly against the important.

When urgency was introduced, 31.3% chose task A when compared to just 13.3% when both tasks were deemed to have the same amount of time.

Urgency trumps the important.

The researchers dubbed this term the *Mere Urgency Effect.* And here's why. [14]

Our mind has many roles, but when we are in a tough situation, whether it's an argument, test, performance, negotiation, or social environment, our brain kicks in and does whatever it can to keep us safe.

The brain is a master at staying safe.

It keeps us safe by making whatever *it* is urgent.

Even if it is not an urgent situation, any stress, fear, or indecision will engage the *urgency response.*

In everyday life, marketers utilize time and urgency as a primary sales tactic.

Powerful words that marketing and advertisers use to create a sense of urgency are vast: *Now, Hurry now, Last chance, One time only, Before it's too late, Today only, Limited time, Instant, Don't miss out, Can't wait.*

Marketing thrives on creating a sense of urgency because urgency amplifies the feelings of already wanting something.

Black Friday is predicated on a sense of both urgency and scarcity. When booking a hotel room or flight and you witness only one left, it sparks a sense of urgency. Also, online deals create urgency when the potential buyer is shown how many people are looking at the same hotel room at the same time that you want it. Fear of Missing Out (FOMO) can also enter the psyche when a deadline is arbitrarily set such as *"if you order now, then you can get it today."*

There exists a tension and discomfort regarding tasks that appear urgent. It affects us all because urgency is the spark that ignites the action bias.

When things appear urgent, we act.

The goal is often simply to remove the discomfort or tension that exists from urgent items. Think about the urgent "code reds" that may take place in your own daily life. These short-term urgencies possess extreme power. It is those stressful, triggering, anxiety-producing, thought-racing moments that occur. There are different situations for many of us, but they still occur to all of us.

Think for instance about what happens inside of our own minds when we lose an object and are obsessed with finding it. It becomes the most important thing ever, and urgency results. And urgency is even more amplified especially if what we have misplaced is needed right now!

— — —

On the PGA Tour, on any given week, I'll speak to many caddies. One of the topics that I ask about is the most important conversations between a pro and caddy.

The same answer continually arises, and research has supported that good caddying is *all about timing* and great caddying is *about great timing.* [15]

Parenting, coaching, and marriage are just like caddying as well. The art is knowing when to say something and when to say something. Are we able to let the situation, issue, or problem unfold, or do we intervene?

I can't wait to be patient.

With our kids, one rule in our home is that we do not talk about the game on the "Car Ride Home." It was a staple in the book, *Don't Should on Your Kids: Build Their Mental Toughness.* However, I broke this covenant after my daughter's soccer game. The game had ended and we were leaving, but I had one brilliant point that I needed to tell my daughter. Urgency was ruling the moment.

It was a small correction that she needed to hear. My wife reflected my own words back to me, *"remember, not during the 'car ride home'."* The instruction that I needed to tell my daughter was so transformative, so enlightening, and life-changing that when we got home, I completely forgot what I was going to say.

Life is about timing, and a great life is about great timing.

Too often, it isn't that the message is incorrect, it is just incomplete because urgency trumps the important.

For instance, your significant other often shares information so he/she can be heard. They share to connect, not for us to chime back with sage advice, *"well, you know what you need to do is..."*

Even though we like to be the problem solver to an urgent situation, we often just need to listen. Less is better.

This is the crux of *I can't wait to be patient.*

Our feedback is probably correct, however, the timing of the solution is way off. We want to be problem solvers and relish in that role, but it's like wanting to tell someone how a magic trick works. If we share the secret and they don't want to know, it is defeating.

Jeff Van Gundy, former NBA head coach, shared one of his communication strategies at a conference. When commenting about his teams, he said, *"we talk about all stressful situations in non-stressful environments."* He didn't want a discussion *in the heated moment* of the game about what the play was, or who was taking the final shot with five seconds remaining on the clock. All of these stressful situations were addressed the evening before, at dinner, for example.

The importance of timing extends to work and life as well.

For instance, let's say you receive an important message in the evening about a project, concern, or item from a coworker, teammate, or superior. This is a situation that "could wait" until the next morning to address, however, your sense of urgency kicks in and we can't wait to be patient.

We act upon the urgent.

Sometimes, it is simpler to reply and address the issue, but it may also come at a cost. How many small fires or messages can we handle before it starts to impact our own mentality and peace? If we address the issue, then we have also communicated that we are open and available at any time to solve "the issue." When we operate that everything is urgent, without time boundaries, it trains the mind to stay in high alert.

More so, when there is a perceived sense of urgency, our attention focuses away from the important tasks and only onto the urgent.

In our own lives, when we *can't wait*, we operate with the belief that action in each and every circumstance has to be better than inaction.

When stressed and facing an unsure outcome, urgency without clarity makes it difficult to rest, observe, evaluate, slow-down, research, converse, journal, breathe, pray, and/or meditate on the situation.

Urgency without a clear focus inhibits our ability to pause and simply think.

Our impulse is to not slow down and reflect, but instead, act quickly.

When we are doing too much, or have too many unfinished projects, or running around, stress or anxiety is the result. Since it requires a level of focus to address urgent issues, it can take away from the focus needed for more important tasks.

Fatigue, clutter, and distractions are killers to the important. They create urgency without teaming up with the important. Stress results when pressured with unrealistic deadlines, follow-ups, or emails, and urgency can easily wane into disengagement and apathy. When we are not aligned with the important, then urgency trumps the important and we become misaligned.

Urgency sparks us to act.

We switch lanes in traffic or change lines at the checkout line. If we are in a line and it stops, the level of impatience can readily be witnessed. If faced with poor outcomes in business or sports, we make changes. We don't examine and evaluate our process as much as we just make a change and see how it goes. Or perhaps we continually "follow-up" with people to see about their progress and completion date.

Per our financial investments, we overtrade or sell during low periods. We bombard our financial advisor to inquire what "actions" they have done. And we overbid during auctions to avoid the potential future disappointment of not winning. And these are just some of the common examples of our action bias with urgency. Performance suffers if we do not pair the important with the urgent.

We need a different approach to combine the important with the urgent. This couple when done correctly allows us to be successful without the stress and angst and it is accomplished not through hacks or five steps, but just through our relationship with time.

"Important urgencies" are when we act with a sense of urgency toward the important. It means acting with clarity of purpose and clear direction on the important tasks.

Founder of Alcoholics Anonymous

Bill Wilson's parents abandoned him and his sister as youths. He suffered from depression and as a twenty-year-old had his first alcoholic drink. He claimed, *"I had found the elixir of life."* He experienced seventeen years of destitute drunkenness and underwent four different hospital stays for alcohol addiction. His comeback resulted in his ultimate sobriety, founding Alcoholics Anonymous (AA), and writing the Big Book of AA. It has since sold over 30 million copies and Bill W. was considered one of the top 100 influential people of the 20th century.

Important urgencies

"Most of us spend too much time on what is urgent and not enough time on what is important."
— Steven Covey

Seth Greenberg spent twenty-two years as a Division I head basketball coach. He was a two-time ACC coach of the year and an ESPN TV analyst and broadcaster. I was speaking with him at a clinic and he commented about how the entire basketball show was organized in terms of content.

He said, *"Whatever is least important goes toward the end of the show, because it's no big deal if we don't get to it."*

Simple…

The most important step is deciding what is most important.

Bill Gates and Warren Buffet were both asked to write down one word that helped account for their success. They each wrote down the same word, which was *focus*.

Jim Collins, author of *Good to Great*, saw that most people and businesses failed by having too many priorities. He believed having more than three priorities meant in reality that you didn't have any. If everything is the most important thing, then we haven't figured out what is most important.

Once we know what is important, the struggle becomes to keep the main thing, the main thing. Because there are so many attention grabbers for our time, we'll need to consistently revisit the important and connect it with our vision, *"Is the decision today or right now important toward the long-term?"*

But, even when we know the destination, we can get stuck in traffic. And I hate traffic jams.

We intuitively know what's important, but numerous distractions exist because of the rapid speed, responsibilities, busyness, and frantic pace that control the short-term.

Life humbly demands for us to adjust. A sailboat is off-course 99% of the time. A sailboat can't directly sail into the wind, but they reach the destination by tacking, making small adjustments along the way. They make zigzagging maneuvers that allow the boat to use both the water current and wind direction to reach the end target.

The headwinds we face during the day can cause us to stay off course if we don't make small adjustments.

Herein lies the balance. We need to be able to trust that vision of the important. However, know that it might not pay off tomorrow, or next month, or even next year. Life pays you back when it wants to, not when you want it to.

I can't wait to be patient...

Success grows in those who know what is important, and act with urgency toward the important. Peace rests with those who are also patient with the results.

The reason why knowing and trusting "the important" matters is because urgency possesses so much power that it trumps the important, and dominates our time, unless we stay focused.

The Stanley Cup

Ray Bourque entered the NHL in the 1979-80 season for the Boston Bruins. Throughout his 21-year Hall Of Fame career, he held the record for most goals, assists, and points by a defenseman. During his final game in the NHL, he won the Stanley Cup with the Colorado Avalanche. He played in 1,612 regular season and 214 playoff games before winning the ultimate prize, which was the longest span in the history of the Stanley Cup.

Four Threats To "Important Urgencies"

*"We should not let an illusion of urgency force us
to make decisions before we are ready."*
— Nelson Mandela

I f *urgency* were a person, it would go alone. Per urgency, the opening line of the African proverb rings true, *"if you want to go fast, go alone."*

Urgency is powerful because we can be urgent towards anything. Although, mistakes are made when we are urgent toward too many things and an overflow of stress and anxiousness results.

If urgency were an animal, it would be a lone wolf. The lone wolf makes up only about 15% of the wolf population. But the lone wolf actively seeks a partner to start a new pack.

Just like the lone wolf, urgency is best when joined with a partner. Urgency needs to be yoked with *the important. The important* is the rudder of focus; it determines the direction of our urgency.

Then, when paired together, the second line of the African proverb rings true: *"if you want to go far, go together."*

Urgency and Importance= Important Urgencies. This combination is as powerful as milk and cookies.

And just like the wolf, even though it's an apex predator, there are still threats. The threats to *Important Urgencies* are often well hidden, but they cause *"I can't wait to be patient."* There are four threats to important urgencies, which are: inefficiencies, excess time, law of triviality, and panic.

I can't wait...to have a magnificent navy...on land

"The days are long, but the years are short."

The origins of the fleet of the United Kingdom's "Royal Navy" began in the 16th century.

The Royal Navy served of vast importance into exploration and discovery across the globe. Up until that period, however, the "king's fleet" was eloquently, yet haphazardly, pieced together.

At the conclusion of World War I in 1918, the Royal Navy had a larger fleet than the United States and French Navy combined.

However, during the period after The Great War, The Royal Navy experienced the largest cutback ever in both funding and ships. There was no urgency and due in part to legislation and peacetime, the Royal Navy severely contracted.

Between 1918 and 1928, the number of Royal Navy officers reduced 31% from approximately 146,000 to 100,000 officers. The number of capital ships *(e.g., the most important ships)* in commission reduced almost 67% from sixty-two to twenty ships.

However, an interesting phenomenon occurred during the major diminishment of both the Royal Navy ships and officers.

Despite the massive reduction in officers by one-third and ships by two-thirds, there was an *increase* in dockworkers, clerks, and *"admiralty officials."*

It was not a slight increase either.

Dockworkers increased by 40% from 3,200 to 4,500 workers. And there was a staggering 78% increase in admiralty officials from 2,000 to 3,500 officials.

While the waters were calm, there were big waves inside of the offices. The staff grew exponentially even though the needs of the Royal Navy were reduced.

Inefficiencies resulted in a magnificent navy…on land. Inefficiencies are the first threat to important urgencies.

The majestic increase in administration, simultaneous with the decrease in sailors and ships, was not lost on some scholars fascinated by the development.

Cyril Parkinson was a naval historian and scholar. Having served in the British military, he was intrigued by the inefficiencies and bureaucracies within administration and management. What began as a satire morphed into scholarly work and in 1957, *Parkinson's Law* was birthed into existence. [16]

Parkinson's Law explained the inefficient bureaucracy of the Royal Navy by showing precisely how the growth took place. Foremost was that *"officials created work for each other."*

He explained that people hired subordinates to assist with deadlines, administration, tasks, and so on. These said individuals were not in direct competition with one another, but over time, their own responsibilities grew.

Hence, more people were hired in order to assist those who were assisting. People needed to be relevant and in short, people created more work for one another, which at some point morphed into grave deficiencies.

In present day organizations, others create work for each other. Meetings, committees, task forces, and initiatives with fancy names simply lead to more work created for one another. It appears beneficial, but deficiencies eventually result. One executive in a large corporation calls it the DSR group, "Desperately seeking relevance."

In regard to time, performance, and productivity, a simple quote emerged from Parkinson's Law that indirectly addressed *important urgencies.*

"Work expands to fill the available time for its completion."

If time is unlimited, then we will take an unlimited amount of time to finish the task.

However, if there is a deadline or time constraint, we will finish the goal in the allotted time. Deadlines or realistic time constraints create important urgencies, which ultimately lead to increased production and efficiency.

It's amazing how productive most people are the week before a vacation!

The week before a vacation is the essence of urgency. People have a to-do list of everything they need to accomplish and since there is no "tomorrow," they simply get the work done.

Survey research of 1,000 office workers revealed that 32% of people's productivity increased the week before a holiday compared to 22% who felt less productive! [17]

Hall of Fame quarterback Roger Staubach went to the Naval Academy where he won the Heisman Trophy. Serving as a midshipman, few can appreciate the difficulty of the discipline, sacrifice, and effort required to succeed. It also demands close connection, cohesion, and reliance on fellow midshipmen.

That said, Roger Staubach admitted that he made his best grades during the busiest of football seasons while at the Naval Academy. The tight schedule, urgency, and focus on the important that was required to be successful led to efficiency.

Advertisers utilize the mere urgency effect because they understand that if people are given as much time as needed, then they won't buy.

Researchers tested the phenomenon of Parkinson's Law and whether *work expanded to fill the amount of time available.*

Aronson and Landy from the University of Texas created an in-lab experiment to test out the hypothesis of "excess time." [18]

The experiment consisted of arranging items for participants to complete. Participants were given simple, identical tasks and were split into two groups.

One group had five minutes to complete the task and the second group was "accidently" provided fifteen minutes to complete the same task.

Participants who only had five minutes (300 seconds) spent an average of 288 seconds on the successful completion of the task.

Those individuals who had fifteen minutes (900 seconds) to complete the task took an average of 640 seconds to complete.

Those who had no urgency and were provided excess time actually utilized more time. The same task was deliberately made longer due to the "excess time" available.

The experiment revealed that Parkinson's Law certainly held true. When there is no urgency, work expands to fill more available time.

The second threat of important urgencies was *excess time.*

Excess time

"Someday never comes."
— John Fogerty

There appears to be two games within an entire sixty-minute NFL game. There's the fifty-six-minutes of the game, and the final two-minutes of each half.

The two-minute offenses (e.g., hurry-up offense) are implemented to achieve one goal, scoring. It is less about scheme and getting first downs and more about the ability to operate with urgency, coupled with poise, and the ability to adapt.

And it works…

Victor Hugo, author of the famous novel, *The Hunchback of Notre Dame*, was plagued by *excess time*. In 1829, he agreed with his publisher to produce the famed novel in twelve months. Yet he was plagued by indulgence, as he was known for hosting dinner parties for thirty or more guests almost every night. In the summer of 1830, he removed excess time and immersed himself into his writing by locking himself into his home, outfitted with only a shawl to wear. His classic novel was written and published within six months.

Scott Jones's business ventures throughout the years made him a multi-millionaire by the age of twenty-eight. He was also relentless with removing distractions from his work. He and his team practically didn't leave the building for two years during the invention and release of a brand new product at the time called *voicemail.*

Excess time is a killer to the important.

Think of a recent important deadline that you had. Chances favor that you met that deadline.

And often, we became more focused and dialed as the deadline approached. Perhaps we even waited until we felt the urgency and were forced to do so, per the deadline. Of course, waiting until the last minute brings in more errors and stress, but if we wait until the last minute, it usually only takes a minute.

In theory, if we prepare and work for four hours, the results will be better than preparing or working for two hours. However, how efficient, productive, focused, and distraction-free are those four hours? Did we address email, answer texts, hop on a call, or watch a quick video?

If a call were scheduled for thirty minutes, there wouldn't be a lot of personal fodder about the weekend, weather, or fantasy football. There would be built-in urgency and the action would represent focus.

Whereas, if a call was scheduled to last an hour, then much more time would be spent discussing additional topics.

A research study of procrastination involved eighty-five students. They were given only specific time windows to study for an exam. The attitude of the students went from *"I have to"* to an attitude of *"I'm allowed to."*

The restriction of excess time increased the learning efficiency and severely limited any sort of procrastination. [19]

President Woodrow Wilson was once asked about how long it took for him to prepare a speech. He replied in a similar vein of excess time. He stated,

> *"If it is a ten-minute speech it takes me all of two weeks to prepare it; if it is a half-hour speech it takes me a week; if I can talk as long as I want to it requires no preparation at all. I am ready now."*

The cause of excess time was born out of another threat of *important urgencies*. It was the law of triviality.

The law of triviality

"Busy is the illusion of control."

In the study of excess time there was a tendency to use more time than needed on *the unimportant* rather than *the important*.

What directed the sense of urgency was not the important, but it was the unimportant details or tasks.

Parkinson cited an example of the design and building of a nuclear power plant. A group of individuals wasted time on unimportant but easy to complete tasks such as deciding the color of the bike shed. [16]

The group did not maximize time on the important and difficult decisions such as the actual design of the power plant itself.

Parkinson argued that work expands to fill the time available because people simply became stuck on the trivial issues.

The law of triviality.

People involved with a task will take an inordinate amount of time on less important or trivial tasks. There may even be urgency, but the unimportant is steering the ship.

The trivial can be witnessed in how we use our time. The intention of your time and the use of time need to match up. Time audits are painful because they reveal how much of our time is wasted on the trivial or unimportant.

For instance, if your goal is to acquire a property, but a majority of your time is spent answering emails or inside of meetings, then the intent and usage of your time does not match.

Learning to hesitate

"The day the seed is planted is not the same day the fruit is eaten."
— Fabienne Fredrickson

In seminal research of decision-making, Dr. Ambroise Descamps and colleagues found a common theme in how people make decisions. [20]

They found that when uncertainty exists about an outcome, the decision maker attempted to reduce the uncertainty by looking for information.

In our own lives, this behavior holds true as well. We seek out as much information as possible if we are searching for reviews about a hotel to stay or seeking out a financial advisor.

The researchers found, however, that people quickly deviated from optimal strategies of decision-making.

When gathering information was costly, people hesitated too long and oversampled information. The optimal strategy was to instead collect only a little information and make a decision.

On the opposite end, when gathering information was readily available, people under-sampled information, when the optimal strategy was to collect a lot of information before a decision.

Since they were unsure about outcomes, they were *"learning to hesitate."*

Big decisions often require collecting an optimal amount of information. A critical mistake for the small decisions is to think for too long and get stuck on the small issues. [20]

The law of triviality crushed a sense of important urgencies.

McKinsey Global Survey of over 1200 managers across a variety of companies revealed that fewer than half of all decisions were made in a timely manner. Sixty-one percent reported that half of the time, the decision making process was ineffective, even though a correlation existed between faster decisions and good decisions. [21]

Too often, trivial issues or unimportant details bog us down. And since we have a limited amount of mental energy and stamina, we can get stuck. It can put us into a negative cycle of action without traction and deplete our important resources needed for the important.

Action without traction

"Never mistake activity for achievement."
— John Wooden

Water that flows down a river or stream does not pick its own path; it instead forges a path. And it *always* forges a path of least resistance. Water goes around branches, rocks, and any other obstructions to keep flowing.

We are the same way. We are designed to get from point A to point B as quickly and efficiently as possible. The shortcoming is that we also forge the path of least resistance. We want to obtain the desired results with as little effort as possible.

And because we seek the path of least resistance, our mind stays engaged on easier rather than more strenuous tasks.

Spending time on trivial matters is actually revered by the mind. As long as the mind is engaged, it is satisfied even though it is a not-important task. It's the mind's job to keep us safe and it does so by thinking that we are being productive. The mind does not like to feel unemployed. If it can stay engaged in a task, even if it's meaningless, it is a way to keep us safe.

Unfortunately, performing activities that stimulate does not always increase long-term productivity.

We mistake action for achievement. And we all can succumb to this threat. When we workout, clean the house, or mow the yard for instance, we feel a sense of accomplishment and immediate gratification. We think, "yep, done!"

And this feeling of gratification is contagious and we seek that feeling of accomplishment, completeness, and self-worth during everyday life.

The harder and longer lasting work that needs to be accomplished or addressed often gets set aside for more urgent tasks.

If it's a group or team meeting, then we feel the need to engage, participate, and make an impact. The meeting may have been successful, but what was really implemented after the meeting? Many executives have even reported having multiple meetings on the same exact topic.

Whenever we are not in control of our time, we pay for it. We can become stuck with the business of life. The appointments, kids' activities, meetings, replying to and deleting emails, traveling, and putting out small fires and code reds for so much of the day that little gets accomplished.

If we are not in control of our time, or have not created enough margin in life, then our schedule will often be filled with randomness, urgency, and complexity.

It becomes action without traction.

Panic — the nasty side of urgency

"When in doubt, run around, scream and shout."
— Herman Wouk

Panic is an intense fear in which one becomes obsessed by the threat at hand. Whether real or perceived stress, panic interferes with proper attention to the task at hand.

Panic results in the *inability to think clearly* in stressful situations.

For scuba divers, panic is the top cause of death. Drowning is listed as the fate, but panic was either the leading cause or contributing cause. Panic has been noted in 68% of all underwater incidents. [22]

Dive conditions, situational, or equipment problems are top concerns.

Situations during underwater diving can quickly change and hence the rapid onset of panic. For instance, one might attempt to ascend to the surface and suddenly experience inadequate buoyancy control and panic can set in.

Panic causes the brain to morph into stressful frantic behavior in an attempt to survive. When this rapidly occurs, thinking ability deteriorates.

Most divers who reported panic underwater have successfully navigated it. 54% relied on their training and readiness to get them through the ordeal. [22]

Panic underwater is life threatening. Above water, however, panic can cause and serve as a contributor to severe performance declines and even health issues.

Panic can be triggered by an extreme amount of stress, a big event, competition, or project, and/or client struggles. Panic stems from having too many tasks, getting behind on deadlines, sacrificing the important for the unimportant, not maintaining self-care, and/or dealing with a major setback.

Urgency is not panic. Urgency is best served up hot, but on a cool plate of calm.

Panic is the inability to think clearly in stressful situations. As a leader or competitor, *panic is highly detrimental to success.*

Uncertainty about the future and how things will unfold can cause us to act. We make rash or hurried decisions when under duress or in times of crises.

When performance suffers, the reaction from leaders is again to act, to change something, anything, in hopes that change will fix it. Change isn't bad, but when on the heels of setbacks and adversity, doing something is not always better. This type of reaction often causes one to "fix" everything instead of pausing, evaluating, and using time. These are the times to be patient.

Plus, when someone in charge of a situation panics, it immediately causes others to panic. It puts people in defensive mode to protect and worry more about themselves and possible implications rather than the solution.

Panic breeds more panic.

When our own actions, emotions, facial expressions, voice tone, and volume become hurried and stressed, our words matter much, much less.

People can sense and interpret panic from these signs and internalize it and spin out panic on their own end.

In our own lives, urgency can turn into panic when we are not in control of our time. Urgency toward the important is good, however panic toward the important can be fatal.

Unfortunately, when people panic toward the trivial, a nasty concoction emerges.

Seventy-seven minutes...

"A moment of patience in a moment of anger can
save a hundred moments of regret."
— Elbert Hubbard

In the most tragic of situations, threats to important urgencies can have awful consequences. In the following example, one can witness the inefficiencies, which contributed to a lack of urgency.

On May 24th, 2022, in a town of approximately 15,000 people, another tragic active shooter situation took place at Robb Elementary School in Uvalde, Texas. [23]

At 11:28 am, the shooter crashed his truck into a ditch across from the school and started shooting at concerned bystanders who approached the wrecked truck.

Armed with an AR-15 assault rifle and a vest full of ammunition, he walked towards Robb Elementary School.

A teacher who saw the crash and the approaching gunman called police at 11:29 am. At 11:30 am, the U.S. Marshalls received a call for assistance from Uvalde Police department in response to the shooting.

At 11:32 am, the shooter was outside of the school and fired his weapon toward the building. One minute later, he was inside of the building. He casually walked down the hall and entered two different rooms, rooms 111 & 112, in which the majority of the heartbreaking shootings would take place.

Three minutes later, at 11:35 am, three Uvalde police officers entered the building followed immediately by three more officers and one county deputy sheriff. Synchronistical, Chief Pete Arredondo entered the building along with two additional Uvalde Consolidated Independent School District Police Officers and five more Uvalde police officers. It was an immediate response time, because a total of nine law enforcement officers were inside of the school within three minutes of the shooter entering.

Upon the officers inside of the school and moving down the hallway towards the shooter, two officers were shot with "grazing" wounds from the active shooter and the officers retreated back down the hallway.

The following are detailed transcripts from the police. [23]

At 11:37 am, Eva Mireles, who was a fourth grade teacher inside one of the rooms of the shooting, messaged her husband, Officer Ruben Ruiz, who was also inside of the elementary school. She messaged him that she was shot. Unfortunately, she would die later en route to the hospital.

At 11:40 am, Chief Arredondo called the landline of the Uvalde Police Department. Arredondo called the landline using his cellphone because he did not have his police or school radio with him. This unfortunately would be a factor into the poor communication processes throughout the ordeal.

Body camera footage revealed an officer stating, *"We believe that he is barricaded in one of the offices, there's still shooting."* Dispatch asked if the door was barricaded, to which a Uvalde officer replied, *"I am not sure, but we have hooligan [a door-entry device] to break it."*

At 11:53 am, Eighteen minutes after law enforcement had entered the school, someone questioned whether there were still kids inside, to which the DPS special agent responded, *"If there is, then they just need to go in."*

At 12:03 pm, a student from inside of the classroom with the active shooter called 911 that lasted twenty-three seconds.

At 12:10 pm, the same student called back and said that there are multiple dead inside. Meanwhile, the first group of deputy U.S. Marshals arrived from Del Rio, Texas, nearly 70 miles away.

At 12:11 pm, Chief Arredondo requested a master key.

At 12:16 pm, the student called again and reported, *"Eight to nine students are still alive."*

Arredondo is recorded saying, *"I just need a key,"*

At 12:17 pm, Chief Arredondo stated, *"Tell them to f----- wait. No one comes in."*

At 12:19 and 12:21 pm, another student called from room 111 and shots were heard over the call.

At 12:21 pm, Chief Arredondo stated, *"Can you go get a breaching tool? Like for a trailer house?"*

At 12:24 pm, Chief Arredondo tried to communicate with the shooter through the wall in both English and Spanish. There was no reply.

At 12:25 pm, a female from inside a classroom told the police dispatcher, *"I got shot!"*

At 12:28 pm, Chief Arredondo stated, *"There is a window over there, obviously. The door is probably going to be locked. That is the nature of this place. I am going to get some more keys to test,"*

"These master keys aren't working here, bro. We have master keys and they're not working,"

At 12:30 pm, almost one hour since the shooter entered the school, Chief Arredondo stated, *"OK. We've cleared out everything except for that room…but, uh, we're ready to breach but that door is locked."*

At 12:38 pm, Arredondo attempted to speak with the shooter through wall in both English and Spanish. Again, there was no reply.

At 12:42 pm Chief Arredondo claimed, *"We're having a f------ problem getting into the room because it is locked. He's got an AR-15 and he's shooting everywhere like crazy. So, he's stopped."*

He continued, *"They gotta get that f------ door open, bro. They can't get that door open. We need more keys or something,"*

At 12:43 pm, a student called from inside room 112 asking police to enter.

At 12:47 pm, the student asked again for police to be sent in.

At 12:50 pm, Paul Guerrero led a border patrol tactical unit team, breached the door, shot and killed the shooter in classroom 111. A key was used; however, it was later disputed that the door may not have been locked.

Unfortunately, within such a harrowing event, the worst can be witnessed:

The shooter was inside of the school for a total of seventy-seven minutes. One hour and fourteen minutes passed from the time the police entered the building until the shooter was stopped.

The shooter entered the classrooms with 315 cartridges of ammunition and fired 142 of them. Nineteen third and fourth graders, and twenty-one people in total, died in the horrific mass shooting.

It was a devastating event that transpired at Robb Elementary School.

There were 376 law enforcement members who responded to the Texas elementary school shooting. However, it was considered the worst response by law enforcement to a mass shooting in U.S. history. Some of the descriptors used to describe the response to the events were "abject failure," "systemic failure," and "egregiously poor decision making."

Even though it was an emergency, the combined threats that emerged sadly led to a lack of urgency.

The factors involved included inefficiencies of both communication and leadership, the law of triviality (i.e., keys), coupled with panic, and perceived excess time (i.e., barricaded suspect). Regrettably, all of these threats manifested into a lack of important urgency from law enforcement at Robb Elementary School.

— — —

According to law enforcement doctrine, the first action by officers, no matter the rank, should be to "stop the killing."

Officers in Nashville, Tennessee, Sergeant Jeff Mathes, Det. Michael Collazo, and Officer Rex Engelbert, acted "without hesitation" to the emergency at The Covenant School on March 27th, 2023.

In stark contrast to Robb Elementary, the active shooter entered the school at 10:10 am and was killed by police at 10:25 am. Sadly, six people were killed, but many other lives were saved due to the heroic urgency of the police officers.

The Path of Patience

"Patience is not an absence of action.
It is a purposeful choice to wait."
— Salman Ahktar

Path (noun): The course or direction in which a person or thing is moving. A way of life, conduct, or thought.

El Capitán is a beautiful rock formation in Yosemite National Park. It's 3000 feet above the floor, which is more than twice the size of the Empire State Building. It has a rich history for expert climbers. The incredible documentaries *The Dawn Wall* and *Free Solo* both took place at El Capitán.

Tommy Caldwell and Kevin Jorgeson in 2015 became the first to successfully summit the toughest route, The Dawn Wall of El Capitán. It is considered one of the pinnacles of climbing history. It took several years of planning and nineteen days of actual climbing to reach the top.

The harder the path we take, the greater the risk, but the greater the reward as well.

There are approximately 252 climbing routes on El Capitán.

Because there are so many different paths we can take, we are often uncertain on the path to choose.

During his acceptance speech for winning Best Actor at the 86th Oscars, Matthew McConaughey spoke frankly of not being able to actually reach the mountaintop.

In his speech, he remarked how at age fifteen, he realized his hero was himself, but ten years into the future. So, when he reached age twenty-five, he knew he wasn't even close to achieving that goal. At age twenty-five, his real hero was himself, but ten years from that point, at age thirty-five.

He knew he was never going to reach the mountaintop destination. And that it was okay it was unattainable, because it always gave him someone to chase.

The point to the story and mountaintop analogy is that there's no wrong one way. We can dive into bettering our lives in tons of different actions and paths. Since there is no wrong path, we end up choosing too many paths.

The problem isn't choosing the right way; it's choosing one way.

This path is about improving your relationship with time. This is the path of patience.

— — —

The mental game is more often about subtraction than it is addition.

That's because it's way harder to remove something in our lives than it is to add something.

Forbearance: To hold back, abstain, to go without, and to control oneself when provoked.

To use a skiing analogy, these actions of forbearance all appear to be double-black diamonds in terms of difficulty. I'd argue they are probably the hardest hitting actions one could take because they entail subtraction rather than addition.

However, we improve exponentially when we remove things, people, ideas, habits, or places in our lives that serve little purpose or make us worse.

Removing anger, frustration, fear, and/or annoyances from our daily lives is difficult. However, doing so also improves our disposition, grit, and attitude. More importantly, patience also builds up one's capacity to handle and endure future disappointment, rejection, and failure.

Patience is the ultimate trainer and test of subtraction.

To illustrate, parenting is both the hardest test and greatest teacher of patience. In that, going through the process of parenting not only reveals our level of patience, but also increases a parent's patience as well.

Because of the importance, power, and relativity of time, patience is the path. It allows us the space and time to decide what's most important and uncover what is of less importance.

This path of patience embodies an increased awareness of time, a relationship with the important urgencies, and an elimination of the stress, worry, and hurry that we carry with us.

With patience, our entire attitude and outlook will change.

Patience is so important, that almost all religions consider patience the highest of virtues. Every faith fosters an admiration for patience.

Islam and the Qur'an 39:10 states, *"Only those who are patient shall receive their rewards in full..."*

In Hinduism, ancient literature refers to patience as pariksaha. Hinduism refers to ten separate sources of patience and forbearance.

Buddhist scripture within the Dhammapada refers, *"enduring patience is the highest austerity."*

Taoism and founder Lao-Tzu believed, *"I have just three things to teach: simplicity, patience, compassion. These three are your greatest treasures."*

Judaism upholds patience as a prominent theme. The word *patience* is mentioned approximately seventy times in the Bible according to translations. The Hebrew Torah, both written and oral, provides several proverbs that extol patience. For example, Psalm 37:7, *"Be still before the Lord and wait patiently for him."* Within the Jewish text of the Pirkei Avot, it is written, *"to be patient in judgment."*

Within Christianity, patience is viewed as a fruit of the spirit. In that, it is a gift from God. Galatians 5:22-23 states, *"But the fruit of the spirit is love, joy, peace, patience, kindness, goodness, faithfulness, gentleness, and self-control."* Romans 12:12 states, *"We are asked to be patient in affliction."*

Perhaps the various faiths put an emphasis on patience as a virtue because we lack the constitutional capability to do it on our own without help and guidance.

Twelve Years After Being Drafted

Jack Campbell was a hockey goaltender and was the eleventh overall pick in the 2010 NHL draft. He played two NHL games over the next seven years with five different teams. He was mired in the minor leagues until 2018 when he won his first NHL game. He became a starter and was selected for the 2022 NHL All-Star team, twelve years after being drafted.

Do you have a patient personality?

"Two of the greatest warriors are patience and time."
—Leo Tolstoy

People with patience seem to be like the sacred Hindu cow. They never appear to be in a hurry. They take their time, seem to wait without haste, and have a remarkable peace about themselves.

The Myers-Briggs Type Indicator (MBTI) is a personality test that many people have taken. Approximately 1.5 million individuals take the test every year. [24]

The test provides sixteen different personality categories for individuals. It became available in 1975 and exploded in popularity. Its popularity was based on the results being seemingly positivist in nature, meaning, it merely provided positive insight without judgment.

The results of the test are clever and used to match certain archetypes of an individual. Some of these "types" include the entrepreneur, the diplomat, the leader, the mediator, etc. The validity of the test, however, has not held up when used as a predictor of future career success.

Nonetheless, it still can be effective as a tool for personal insight and awareness. The aspect of the test worth noting, however, can provide immense benefit and insight. Hyperbole aside, it can be life changing.

It is the last letter of our results that provides an indicator of how we organize our outer world. Everyone is labeled as either a "J" or a "P".

Do you prefer your day to be more planned and structured, or more spontaneous and flexible?

Now, society has dictated our schedules somewhat, because we have to be at certain places or appointments at specific times.

In life, we can find exceptions to this question of whether we prefer structure or flexibility. There is a lot of gray and we can be in the middle for much of this question.

So, think of a day off or vacation. Do you like to have a plan or see what unfolds? Are you one of the people who love to have a plan for vacation or do you hate the idea of having any plan at all?

This area of our personality has nothing to do with risk-taking, spending habits, talent or ability, being organized, or whether you are introverted or extraverted. It just has to do with whether you like to have a plan or not.

One of these "types" is akin to having patience. If you are planned and structured, then you're a J. However, if you are a P, then you are more adaptable or flexible.

J's prefer control to chaos and they are very decisive, organized, and complete. J's love lists and they love blocking out time for tasks. They will get the job done.

The J's prefer to have a plan and they can operate freely within that plan or schedule. However, what happens to J's when their schedule or plan is altered?

J's are not the personality of patience. J's have an interesting reaction that takes place when their scheduled plan is changed or altered. Abrupt change is the pebble in their shoe. J's will struggle with change, no matter how insignificant.

If there is any shift in the plan such as…

"Do you want to go to lunch?"

"Do you want to go ahead and have that meeting now?"

"Do you have a minute to talk?"

"Can you go throw the ball outside with me?"

Then they will have the same reaction.

J's will complain.

Whether it's an external reaction or not depends upon the person. It doesn't mean that there is a huge, drawn-out gripe session. It's more of a moan session. But J's will nonetheless, complain.

And the reason why they complain even if only a little bit is because something or someone has messed with their schedule, their own plan.

They may complain just for a few brief moments, but they need to re-adjust and re-focus. They need time and space.

Truth be told, I am a J and it's disturbing at times. Yes, I get the job done. But, I simply do not adjust very quickly, unless adjusting was part of the original game plan.

I can't wait to be patient.

If I am working or involved with some other project or task, then I will complain, even about the simplest of requests. When my kids come in, "Hey dad, want to get some ice-cream?" *Moan…*

"Dad, can you make me a sandwich?" *Moan…*

It doesn't matter the situation, I simply need a little time and space to process.

The real issue with J's isn't that they moan and complain; it's whom they are around when it occurs. The struggle can become toxic depending upon whoever is within earshot. Others can get easily sucked into the vortex of negativity.

The main issue is no longer the main issue. Now, we are mired in a "what's wrong," cleanup, dialogue, or stance phase.

For example, my own kids might assume that Dad is moaning and complaining because he doesn't want to get ice cream, or he is in a bad mood. Their perception could lead them to think, *"Maybe I shouldn't bother Dad."*

When in reality, my reaction has nothing to do with the request or them at all, it only has to do with the plan having been altered and Dad needs time and space to process.

That's it. Because the plan or schedule was altered, J's need time and space to process.

Unfortunately, J's are not the personality of patience.

There is hope, however. There's a surefire strategy to deal with J's if you are one, live with one, work or play alongside one. Since they will moan regardless of the change or idea or proposal, the plan is to provide them with the time and space to moan so that you're not drawn into it.

You need to *hit & run.*

Whenever possible, hit them with the idea, plan, change, or invitation and quickly remove yourself from the potential negative air.

Hit & run.

J's will figure *it* out, but during this thinking out loud, moan period, they won't infect you with their lack of being able to immediately adjust.

Here's how it specifically works, for example: when asking, "Do you want to go to lunch?" ask and leave the room. *Hit and run* and allow them time to process and figure it out.

This is also where the technology of text message can effectively deal with J's. Hitting them with information via text message can allow them to process on their own and they are less likely to moan back to you since it takes more energy to do so.

If you're a J and you know it, you must share this with your co-habitants on the *hit & run* technique. It will work wonders!

If J's lack patience, then P's are the preferred personality of patience.

They are flexible, adaptable, and can adjust. P's enjoy learning and are often even seen as more approachable and warm than their fellow J's.

If you're a P, congratulations!

However, P's are not without their own faults and cracks in the pavement. They organize their outer world by going with the flow and it seems wonderful, except when it comes to decision making.

For instance, when P's have to make decisions, it automatically puts them in a planned and structured mode, which is uncomfortable. Hence, when asked if they want to go to lunch, their immediate response is, "YES!" However, when followed up with *where* do they want to go, the answer becomes "I don't know."

P's need options to stay in their free-flowing world; hence they need to be pushed to closure. They need options.

Since they like to stay adaptable and flexible, options provide that freedom.

Hence, back to the lunch example. They are excited to go with the flow to lunch, but instead of asking them for a specific place, give them options of Wendy's or Chick-Fil-A.

Sometimes, P's are so non-committal that they can be asked what they "don't" want. Do you *not* want Mexican or Italian for lunch?

The Oldest Heavyweight Champion

George Foreman won the boxing heavyweight championship in 1973 after beating Joe Frazier. He retired after losing the famous *Rumble in the Jungle* fight to Muhammad Ali. But, in 1994, at the age of forty-five years old and ten months, the unranked Foreman beat Michael Moorer to regain the Heavyweight championship. It was twenty years after his first title and he stated, *"I was the best I ever was at age forty-six! Something I'd waited for, for years. Boxing, sparring, bag punch and roadwork were like a dream."*

We need to know *when* to be urgent and *how* to be patient.

Patience has many layers. It takes time to be patient.

There are four skills in particular on how-to be patient. [25]

— Acceptance of things and people as they are.
— Assurance for a better future.
— Absence of resentment.
— Ability to wait without haste or restlessness.

1) Acceptance of things and people as they are

"Acceptance is the key to all of my problems."
— Bill Wilson

In 1754, in present day United States, *New France* consisted of lands from Canada to the Gulf of Mexico and it included the Great Lakes regions. Britain, on the other hand, possessed the thirteen flourishing colonies.

Both the French and British wanted the land in the current day Ohio Valley. Trading and expansion were big business and the European powers' battle for dominance flowed into the new land.

The indigenous Indians themselves inhabited the same lands for thousands of years and therein laid a complex relationship amongst nations.

George Washington — prior to leading the Continental Army during the Revolutionary War and becoming the first president of the United States — was a young colonel in the Virginia Regiment.

The youthful twenty-two-year-old George Washington was sent on a mission to inform the French of the British intentions to move into the

Ohio Valley. He built a fort in the valley, which would be called *Fort Necessity*. A circular fort, it was meant for supplies, more so than a defensive fort, however, situations quickly changed.

He, proudly and boldly, went on an offensive. A skirmish erupted which became Battle of Jumonville Glen. It resulted in the death of a French officer, Joseph Coulon de Villiers Jumonville. [26]

The French retaliated by sending 600 French and 100 Indians marched toward Fort Necessity and Col. George Washington with his approximately 400 militia and British regulars.

On July 3rd, 1754, at 11:00 am, the French and Indian forces began attacking the fort. Washington in his earliest battle was outnumbered and under heavy attack.

Heavy rain affected the battle that took place and both sides encountered losses. Washington's men became entrenched and due to the heavy rain, their gunpowder was wet and unable to sustain their firefight. Any escape was severed and they were in a dire situation. The French had surrounded and fired onto Fort Necessity for over nine hours.

However, the French commander, Captain de Villiers, also faced a dilemma. They had failed to take the fort and were now low on ammunition themselves. They were also unaware if British reinforcements were coming and their Indian allies in the fight had threatened to leave by the morning.

Hence, the French sent a negotiation for surrender. At 8:00 pm that evening, the fighting was over and around midnight, George Washington capitulated.

It would be the only surrender of George Washington's career. George Washington's command had lost a quarter of his men, either killed or wounded during the fighting. However, the capitulation terms stated that the soldiers could safely leave the fort, keep their guns, and return home with the honors of war.

Although at the time it was a military and diplomatic failure,

it was an act of courage and strength for George Washington to surrender.

He had a realization and *acceptance of the situation as it was*, not as he would have it.

Washington during these years was described as young, brash, and temperamental. But, in this situation, he stood with his men and set aside any reckless ambition and embodied a quality that would serve him well in the future.

Washington was deeply concerned with honor and his reputation. This incident at Fort Necessity hurt his pride and it served as a major learning experience. He was even demoted during this time, and his goal of becoming a commissioned British officer was not to be. Thus, he resigned and regrouped.

Unbeknownst to him, George Washington's skirmish and subsequent Fort Necessity defense was a hinge moment. It initiated the inevitable *French and Indian War*. However, that was just the North American version. It began and encompassed the *Seven Years War*, which was a global war impacting several continents.

It's not about the setback, it's about the comeback.

George Washington's first comeback moment followed the next year in 1755. He served under General Edward Braddock of the British as a voluntary aide. General Braddock led approximately 1300 men toward Fort Duquesne. Despite pleas from Washington on potential surprise attacks from the alliance of the French and Indian forces in the wilderness, Braddock faced disaster.

During the Battle of Monongahela, Braddock's force became outflanked, disoriented, and he ordered a retreat. However, at that moment, General Braddock was struck by a bullet and mortally wounded.

Washington immediately assumed command and for the next two hours survived a hailstorm of bullets to rally the men to escape. To illustrate the severity of the moment and his own constitution of courage, he had two horses shot from underneath him and his jacket had four bullet holes in it.

Washington fought with incredible poise under fire and earned hero status from saving the British army from entire destruction.

— — —

Acceptance is not denial.

Acceptance does not mean approval of or even liking a situation. It does not mean celebrating a setback. Acceptance doesn't mean going out for pizza after a failure. It's not joyfully praising a situation that was not on the level. It isn't congratulating a teammate or coworker for their annoying habit or idiosyncrasy.

Acceptance means facing reality and living life on life's terms.

Eckhart Tolle qualified acceptance as *"surrendering to the moment."*

Acceptance, surrender, and/or submission do not seem like positive states of mind. Remember, it is tougher to remove things in life than it is to add things. Hardly would one look at surrender during an act of war as courageous. But, in dire situations like the one mentioned where defeat is most likely assured and lives are at stake, capitulation is an act of strength and awareness.

Surrender has often saved more lives than outright refusal to accept the situation.

Ask yourself this question, *"does more pain come from letting go or resisting?"*

Acceptance of things and people as they are is difficult. It's why we all get stuck. Not many of us want to accept that we get older, for instance. Not many accept being wrong or changing their mind. Few want to accept death and heartache as part of life. Few want to accept that life is not fair. It is painful to lose material possessions, friends, jobs, houses, money, championships, etc. It's even worse and more difficult to accept when we are cheated or swindled.

Acceptance of change in our life is difficult. Our goals change, our kids change, our finances change, our relationships change, etc. But since time is the only constant, our view and actions within time need to change as well.

We improve when we are willing to use time to our benefit. Patience means to develop a sense of acceptance. We grow as we accept that there is good and bad and many new beginnings result from horrible endings in life.

Since the pandemic, life and especially the business world have changed. People and leaders simply had less control and influence of their products, decisions, and strategies. Supply chain issues, logistics, and rising costs severely disrupted many industries. With the interconnectedness of so many businesses, owners lost control.

The role of leaders immediately became much more demanding and crucial. Backlogs, breakdowns, and the fragility of a workforce suddenly became the norm, and the changes were on top of the already existing expectations of business.

What was once somewhat predictable now turned into everyone having to make continual adjustments. Customers and businesses now had code red emergencies and every customer, partner, and colleague wanted to be first in line.

Patience is the ability to accept people, places, and things as they are, not as we would have them be.

Longest Heir To The Throne

Charles III became King of England at the age of seventy-three. He was the longest serving heir-apparent in the history of the monarchy before becoming king.

---

2) Assurance for a better future

"Most people overestimate what they can do in a year and underestimate what they can do in two or three decades."
— Tony Robbins

Justin Thomas started off the 2021-2022 PGA Tour season helping The United States win the 43rd Ryder Cup. During his next nine events on tour, he had his most consistent stretch of play in his career to date. He had eight top-ten finishes, and he only finished once outside of the top-twenty.

However, the media pointed out that what was lacking at that point in the season was an individual tournament victory.

After he finished tied for 3rd after an event, the fourteen-time PGA Tour winner and major champion had some prophetic words. He said *"It's coming."* He added, *"I've just got to be patient and be in the right frame of mind...so when it does happen, I'm expecting it."* [27]

Not long after these words came The PGA Championship at Southern Hills Golf Course. After a poor third round score of 74 (+4 over par) he was seven shots out of first place and only had a 1.2% chance of winning.

Justin Thomas shot a final round 67 (-3 under par) en route to winning the championship in a playoff.

When Justin Thomas was asked about what stood out in the path to winning his 2nd major championship, he replied *"patience."*

— — —

Confidence is patience.

When the greats in any field know that they have what it takes and are confident in their own process, it provides a level of assurance for a better future.

Confidence means they have an attitude of "when" not "if" the results will manifest.

Confidence and patience work in tandem. When we are confident, we are able to have more patience. And when we are patient, it allows us to be confident.

That is why *an assurance for a better future* is a source of patience. When we are patient with the product, it grants us perspective with the process.

When we "can't wait" and force or manipulate a situation or person, it also reveals our own level of confidence and patience.

We need to be urgent with the process, but patient with the results.

A Major Champion

Sergio Garcia became a professional golfer in 1999. In his career, he had won, to date, thirty-six international professional golf tournaments. However, he was winless in major championships for his first seventy-three attempts since 1999. He won The Masters in 2017, which was his seventy-fourth major appearance.

Urgent with the process, patient with the results

"Hope is a good thing, maybe the best of things, and nothing good ever dies."
—Andy Dufresne (Shawshank Redemption)

Hope, belief, assurance, optimism, and confidence are all close relatives living in the same house. If we have real *assurance for a better future*, then the source of it matters.

Assurance for a better future means that the time spent on important urgencies will *eventually* yield results. Successful individuals are so fanatical about the process that time ultimately produces success.

— — —

Philip Hans Franses of the Erasmus School of Economics analyzed when the best in the creative arts field created their most quality work. He found the age of when the best creatives in writing, painting, and music "peaked." On average, authors who won the Nobel Prize created their best work at age forty-five. Classical composers produced their best works at age thirty-nine. Painters "peaked" at age forty-two. [28, 29]

There were some prodigies who "peaked" early in life in their teens and twenties, but many as well produced their best works in their forties and fifties and beyond.

For instance, Edward Hopper painted his best work, *Nighthawks*, at age sixty, and his most expensive painting sold for 14 million dollars at age eight-three. Nonetheless, throughout his life, he released over 182 artworks.

On the opposite end, composer Charles Ives produced his best work at the age of seventeen years old. However, he also published well over 114 songs during his lifetime and once took six years to compose his Symphony No. 4.

Jimmy Donaldson, better known as MrBeast, started posting YouTube videos in 2012. His original channel in 2013 had 240 subscribers. He spent several years posting before one of his videos had over 1k views. Since then, he has garnered over 23 billion views and has become YouTube's highest earner at $54 million per year.

Not many would cite *patience* as a key component of the greats in history. People would first mention their work ethic, resiliency, and focus toward their craft. They did possess these skills and an extreme sense of urgency toward the important. They all had an innate, almost insatiable quest for improving.

Hall of Fame Coach Lou Holtz described this quest as being *"pleased, but never satisfied."*

The best in any field have all possessed urgency for improvement. They were *urgent with the process.* There was such urgency towards a goal that it would simply fit the clinical definition of *obsessive.*

For instance, Michael Phelps, during his teenage years, swam every single day for a five-year stretch. He would swim on his birthday, Thanksgiving, Christmas, holidays, etc. Every single day, he swam.

Amongst the greats, there was not balance during times of urgency so much as there was total immersion towards getting better.

Kobe Bryant demanded excellence and with that came urgency toward improvement. Kobe Bryant called it being *"impatiently patient."* Michael Phelps's coach Bob Bowman would continually stress focusing on the process, not the outcome.

Thomas Edison, the greatest inventor of all-time was obsessed with the process. Edison's recipe strived for an invention every ten days, and a major invention every six months. Similar to Phelps's obsessiveness was the way Edison also emphasized output over success. He was consumed with a deliberate approach toward consistency.

For example, you have most likely heard the Edison *10,000 attempts* quote in relation to failure and success. But even more impressive was that Edison attempted 50,000 experiments before succeeding at the alkaline battery patent in 1906.

If Edison followed his own formula of an *invention every ten days* then it took approximately fourteen continuous years of attempts before success with the alkaline battery.

Rock and Roll Hall of Fame lead singer of Pearl Jam, Eddie Vedder, was also obsessed with the process. He immersed himself towards creativity and songwriting. He would constantly carry a coil-ringed notebook with him and during urgent moments, he would jot down thoughts, ideas, lyrics, or inspirations.

These examples of some of the best reveal the powerful effect that time has on greatness. They cultivated an assurance for a better future because of their urgency and obsessiveness toward the important.

But, they were all patient with the results.

— — —

"Hope is a dangerous thing, it can drive a man insane."
– Red (*Shawshank Redemption*)

There is a dichotomy of hope.

Time is the great revealer of confidence, but it is finicky. Too often, people have assurance for a better future; however, it is rooted in an optimism that only satisfies the ego. It is more pleasurable to think of good outcomes and positive scenarios than the negative. Hence, many overestimate their chances of success.

For example, more than half of American millennials believe that they will be millionaires. One of five of these said individuals also believe they will achieve the status before the age of forty years old.

The stark reality is that roughly 8% of the population are millionaires. [30]

Recent surveys showed that 26% of parents wanted their children to play sport professionally. They answered it like it was a choice, however, the actual number is that less than 1% will achieve that professional status.

The trend of "overconfidence" continues in many areas:

- 65% of people think that they have above-average intelligence. [31]
- 80% of people rated themselves top of all-drivers. [32]
- Most students judged themselves as "above average" in popularity. [33]

Take entrepreneurship, for instance. Many people think entrepreneurs are unique. And they are different, *at least the successful ones.*

However, it appears entrepreneurs are no different than the general population in that, they also overestimate their chances of success. [34]

We assume that since no entrepreneurs start businesses designed to fail that they must possess a certain level of belief and assurance that they will succeed.

Statistics show that the majority of entrepreneur start-ups fail. Within six years, on average, over 60% have closed. [34]

Confidence is funny. It's not that these individuals weren't confident in their ventures, but their assessment of themselves was simply incomplete.

Adversity, struggle, and setbacks, over time merely *revealed* or *uncovered* one's true level of confidence.

We all want certainty, assurances, and promises in life. However, reaching the destination is not guaranteed. Setbacks and adversity can derail us all. Just because we know the path to take, it does not reveal to us where the path is covered up, the steep cliffs, fallen down trees, or rockslides.

The assurance is that we stay steadfast in the belief for a better future! Václav Havel once stated, *"Hope is a state of mind, not a state of the world!"*

Assurance for a better future is the key term here. If we place our energy and focus on outside events or results, then we are often at the whim of the ups and downs in life. We are at the mercy of our results, statistics, expectations, and other's opinions of us when we place too much focus on the product.

Assurance for a better future requires patience.

"1 Now faith is the assurance of things hoped for, the conviction of things not seen. 2 Faith is the confidence that what we hope for will actually happen; it gives us assurance about things we cannot see." Hebrews 11:1

The Forest Man of India

Jadav Payeng was a teenager when he came across hundreds of washed up snakes on the island of Majuli in India. Thus, in 1979, he began planting trees on the sand bar to combat the erosion. Over forty years, he created a vast forest that now spans over 1300 acres. Today, the island houses over one hundred elephants, a hundred deer, five Royal Bengal tigers, wild boars, several species of birds, including vultures and pelicans, and many one-horned rhinoceroses. The forest is known as Molai forest and he has become known as the forest man of India.

"Even If" Hindered

"Be patient with yourself. Self-growth is tender; it's holy ground."
— Stephen Covey

Even though we are like water and try to find an easier, softer path, a river has one major advantage. A river cuts through rock, not because of its power, but because of its persistence.

When we are urgent with the process and patient with the results, we improve our relationship with time. It becomes our ally and with time, persistence and perseverance can exert their influence.

Perseverance is from the Latin root word of *persevērāre*, which means *to persist and continue steadfastly, even if hindered.*

When we have patience, we allow *time* to work in our favor.

Back to the Justin Thomas example, for instance: he had a "1.2% chance of winning" as he started his final round of the PGA Championship.

He showed perseverance because he was able to stay patient *"even when"* hindered.

The Loveable Losers

The Chicago Cubs won the World Series in 1908, which was the same year the Model T Ford made its debut. They became dubbed the loveable losers and "cursed." After a 108 year hiatus, The Chicago Cubs won the World Series on November 3rd, 2016.

3) Absence of resentment toward others or ourselves

"We don't see things as they are, we see things as we are."
— Anaïs Nin

"*It is what it is*" has become a common phrase that many use as a catchall term. Whenever someone says, "it is what it is," it usually means that something bad happened. I've yet to witness anyone hold up a championship trophy and say, *"Hey, it is what it is."*

Since "*it is what it is*" is used in a negative sense, the term doesn't sit well. It represents defeat. It is used as an endpoint. It is meant in terms of helplessness that we cannot change the negativity or poor outcome.

Even though he suffered defeat and surrendered at Fort Necessity, I failed to come across George Washington's writings of proper English uttering, *"tis what tis."*

When these words are spoken, they've abdicated control and responsibility over the person or situation and shut down any hope to look at the opportunity. Worse, they essentially don't want any of the personal responsibility from "it is what it is" and these words shed them of that role.

And when you have a leader or person of influence utter this phrase, it suppresses an attitude that requires an adaptive and creative mindset.

Unfortunately, their circumstance has become their condition.

That is why George Washington never uttered the words.

The over-used idiom of *"it is what it is"* should be a starting point instead of an endpoint. Defeat and uncontrollable situations will arise, however, it's how we use the words "it is what it is."

If we don't accept situations, circumstances, or people as they are, then the opposite takes place, which is denial, refusal, or rejection.

I've uttered the phrase "that is unacceptable." It could have been about behavior of my own or someone else. In the moment, I did not meet the standards or expectations that I set for myself. However, when something is "unacceptable," it is usually about a short-term situation and remember the short-term is incomplete.

Continued unacceptance ultimately leads to resentments.

We messed up, someone did us wrong, or a loved one disagreed with us and we developed a resentment or contempt toward others or ourselves.

Often, and in unhealthy ways, we blame, complain, and criticize. We post negative reviews, write anonymous emails, lash out on social media, get angry, resentful, and blocked. Much of the time, these are an emotional reaction instead of a well-thought-out response.

Enter the tendency for interpersonal victimhood (TIV). TIV is a result of a lack of patience born from an inability to accept situations as they are.

Researchers have defined it as *a feeling that the self is a victim, which is generalized across many kinds of relationships.*[35]

The individuals who most embody the victimhood mentality are those individuals who you dare never to ask, "How THEY are doing." These are the folks who drone on about how wrong everything is in their life.

The four components of TIV include, *need for recognition, moral elitism, lack of empathy, and rumination.*

- A *need for recognition* is simply that someone else must acknowledge his or her suffering. If no one is there to glorify his or her own victimhood, then TIV dies. However, misery loves company. Many individuals blame, complain, and criticize because of the attention they receive.

- *Moral elitism* is the belief that they are in the right and those on the other side are in fact immoral. One can see it every day; people dig into their trenches with their beliefs and attitudes towards those who disagree.

- A *lack of empathy* is simply a preoccupation of one's own suffering and a lack of concern about others. These individuals live with the ideal that all of life should be fair and just.

- Lastly, *rumination* is an obsessive focus on the symptoms and causes of the issue long after the stressor has ended. Hate has to think and remind oneself about why they are angry or resentful towards someone else.

When we feel like we are not in control over our situation, we perceive events and specific people as threats.

However, when we view time as a threat, time becomes one of the easiest scapegoats for interpersonal victimhood. Hence, the use of the excuse *"I don't have the time."*

Negativity is more powerful than positivity. Hence, negative reviews garner more attention than positive reviews.

Most people that post comments on social media of a company or person are by those who developed resentments! Something unacceptable occurred and they wanted everyone to know about it. Perhaps they wanted something free in return for their trauma and suffering. Often, they felt the customer service simply did not meet their needs.

The "crowd" is fairly smart, and they learned that if a company is put on blast for all to witness, then they would often get a response. Companies have become paranoid over poor reviews. They know it's more powerful to avoid negative reviews than it is to garner positive reviews.

I disliked poor reviews for my books, until I discovered something. I tracked some of the poorest reviews for my books, and saw the reviews they posted for other author's books. Yep! The majority of their reviews were negative as well, so I no longer felt special.

Negative reviews are an interesting phenomenon. We like reviews and we pay more attention to negative reviews because we think, *"this person is being honest and showing us what it's really like!"* We assume the person leaving the review is similar to us, our beliefs, and how we operate. However, we have no idea about the person who posted the negative review. They could be that annoying slow driver who always drives in the fast lane, or the runner who jogs in place at a traffic stop waiting for the light to change. We know nothing about them, but at the same time, we put way too much credence and significance into their negative review.

We think they are actually showing us the wizards behind the curtain, however, reviews often aren't always showing honesty and transparency. They are merely expressing one person's resentment in a public forum.

Unfortunately, individuals with T.I.V. often don't want their problem solved, because that would mean getting rid of their own resentment. Then, they could no longer tell you or everyone else about it. People hold onto their resentments like a backpack because it provides them an outlet for their own insecurities and anger.

——— ——— ———

When I was a senior in high school, we had a gym period in which a group of us would always play basketball. It was always competitive, but friendly. I was a baseball player at my school, so my coach never liked me playing basketball during the gym period, for fear that I would get injured.

One day, there was for some reason a combination of gym classes and a few other guys played with us. When one particular player went up for a shot near the basket, I grabbed his body to keep myself from falling. However, he didn't see it that way. He immediately wanted to fight and in fact called me out in front of everyone to "go." This kid was tough, but he was also into hustling and drugs.

I didn't react because I was shocked and so I backed down. I didn't like to be challenged but I also could not risk getting into trouble. I had a lot more to lose as an athlete. But I was raging inside.

The incident ended and that was it. I don't recall ever conversing with him again. But, I was pissed off. I still felt the rage of being called out.

The sad part is that I held onto that resentment for years! Years!

Whenever I felt stupid or inferior in a situation, I would experience the same feelings as in that high-school gym. It still feels silly to even admit that the gym period would have had such a profound impact.

I harbored that resentment. I allowed that resentment to take up residence in my own mind. It paid no rent, mind you, because that resentment was a squatter. It was a deadbeat friend who refused to move out, until I had to kick him out.

And my own dreaded resentment had little to do with him. It had more to do with my own childish insecurities.

What occurs when a resentment is formed over a friend, coworker, or loved one with whom we interact and engage with every day?

Today's expectations easily turn into tomorrow's resentment.

Resentment unchecked becomes contempt.

Contempt is the "roll your eyes" type of disgust.

Contempt is sadly the number one predictor for divorce. It is the next level resentment in which one feels disgust toward another.

And if left unchecked, resentment or contempt towards yourself is actually the worst. It limits your full potential. We may continue forward, but we still carry around past failures, guilt, and shame which affect how we look at ourselves. And *we can't outperform our own self-image.*

Conflict will occur, but it we can't find a way to process the anger or situation, then the resentment will form and grow.

An absence of resentment means we have to examine our role in any given situation. We can't change the outcome or other people without understanding our own insecurities and baggage in a situation.

It starts with us.

To possess an absence of resentment means to approach people, situations, and especially ourselves with patience.

If we have resentment toward ourselves for a past setback, then we will develop resentment towards others. It's a simple formula of "arrows in" also means "arrows out."

Hurt people will hurt other people because the cycle of resentment is so powerful. If we don't transform our past pain, then we will transmit it to others closest to us.

In order to be patient, we must develop an absence of resentment towards others and ourselves. When we do this, time again begins to work in our favor and removes that hurt we held onto.

When we let go of *it*, *it* lets go of us.

4) Ability to wait without haste or restlessness

Wisdom says, "wait." Emotions say, "hurry."
— Joyce Meyer

I was golfing with my passionate eleven-year-old son on a summer Friday afternoon. As we teed off, there was a foursome behind us and a foursome in front of us. It was just us, a twosome, so we were nestled in-between these groups.

When we started playing on the back nine however, the foursome in front of us was still on the 10th tee box. *Their food and drink orders at the turn must have taken a bit longer than usual.*

It was fine, however, as we *patiently* waited for that group in front of us to play.

During this waiting period on the tee box, another twosome arrived at the 10th tee box. They were locals to the course and were trying to get nine holes of play in. I knew the situation behind us and in front of us, so I asked if they simply wanted to join us. They agreed.

They were both fine golfers, and the next few holes were enjoyable. However, the 13th and 14th holes were a tad more challenging as the wind had picked up and the holes took longer because one of us had issues.

During this time, the foursome behind us had caught us and now they were waiting on us.

It happens…

However, on the 15th tee box, as we prepared to tee off, one of the guys who joined said to me, "*I told my partner that we should allow this foursome behind us to play through.*"

I didn't reply audibly and kind of shrugged my shoulders as I striped my tee shot down the middle of the fairway. There were several scrambled thoughts going through my head.

- First, there's a social contract within golf. I simply didn't see the need with four remaining holes to allow the foursome behind us to play though.
- Second, the main reason why the foursome behind us was now waiting on us was because we allowed the additional two players to join us.
- Third, we were at the point in the round where some fatigue started to set in, and I wanted to proceed and finish with clarity of mind.
- Fourth, the foursome behind us was still on the previous 14th green.

These were all excuses and rationalizations, mind you, but the truth was, in the actual moment, I couldn't *wait to be patient.*

Remember, I am a "J" personality, and this change was not part of my plan.

After my son struck his tee shot down the middle of the fairway, I looked back to see the foursome still on the 14th green.

I immediately became anxious and overwhelmed. I simply wanted to keep pace and play.

I didn't want to wait.

After thirty seconds of deliberating and being stuck inside of my own head, I waved and told the two players who joined us that we were going ahead. My son and I played fast and were finished the hole as the foursome behind us were finally on the tee box.

As my son and I played the next hole, we resumed our usual standing in the golf pecking order as we easily caught the foursome in front of us.

Emotions say, "hurry."

I couldn't wait to be patient. I'm writing about this story, because I struggle with the ability to wait without haste or restlessness.

What took place was an internal, silent, and emotional battle. I was a victim to my emotions. This wasn't a planned act, and the option to be patient and wait didn't enter my mind.

I didn't operate with a profit and loss balance sheet. I didn't have a patience monitor. I was in play and competition mode and while having fun, I didn't want the flow and rhythm interrupted. My son and I played the final four holes alone and finished about 20 minutes ahead.

The ability to wait without haste or restlessness seems to be the core concept of patience.

We can see when people can't wait to be patient. Impatience is witnessed far easier than patience. It's tough from an outsider perspective to see someone show restraint, unless it's Chris Rock at The Oscars.

However, we feel the impatience of a stressed out boss or coach, someone weaving in and out of traffic, or someone getting annoyed in a checkout line.

— — —

We feel like we can't slow down, because we perceive everything as urgent.

The crux of patience is that we have become *urgent toward the unimportant.* Our emotions and mood tell us that it is important in the short-term, but with time, the urgent cannot be coupled with the unimportant.

For example, in our adult life, when an opportunity to wait without haste or restlessness presents itself, we revert to our phone. It temporarily pacifies us from getting stressed or anxious. However, the phone itself can easily cause stress or anxiety.

We check our phone on average eighty-five to ninety-five times per day and literally unlock the action of the world. *(Some research suggests we unlock our phone 10x that amount)* We live stream, communicate important ideas, trade stocks, buy items, view funny videos, search for romantic partners, order food, and so on.

We don't wait. We scroll…

We delete emails, mindlessly scroll social sites, text others, post videos, etc.

When we awake in the morning, we are often at odds with our own sense of urgency. And this sense of urgency is usually toward the unimportant.

Research has shown that upon waking in the morning, four out of five people check their phones within fifteen minutes. Nearly 80% of people comment that it's the first thing they do in the morning. I'm guilty of it. [36]

And here's what I noticed. If I scroll before I run in the morning, then my mind is hijacked. I've become preoccupied with someone else's highlight reel, news, or comment. It can easily shift my mindset into becoming opinionated, agitated, or feeling a need to get busy.

The first hour of the day, sets the rudder for the rest.

Research of 2250 individuals showed that simple mind wandering occurred almost 47% of the time in people. Our mind wanders about what has occurred in the past, what might occur in the near future, and things that will never happen. The importance of the research was that individuals' happiness depended more on what they were thinking throughout the day rather than what they were actually doing. The more that people's minds wandered, the less happy that they were. Our mind wandering from the important to something more pleasant actually leaves us *less* happy. [37]

The *ability to wait without haste or restlessness* is born from knowing the difference between the important and the unimportant.

When the urgent and unimportant collide, it's a head-on crash!

Research showed that 80% of Americans experienced some sort of technology frustration *every day*. Even though technology has increased the speed in life to get from point A to point B, what occurs when the technology fails to work as expected? [38]

Coincidence, but it always seems the technology issues arise during the most urgent of times.

According to research, a few of the most common technology issues include an inability to connect, remembering or resetting passwords, logging in to your device, and/or slow loading times. [38]

However, think about how rapid the window of time for waiting has become when relying on technology. Recently, at a student/teacher conference, the instructor attempted to show her screen on a projector to all in attendance. It cycled and buffered through, but did not show up immediately. It took about thirty seconds for the teacher's screen to show up accurately, but the frustration was about three seconds before she commented begrudgingly to the parents on the situation. And it wasn't just her; there was a silent expectation for it to load immediately.

Our reliance on technology in relation to impatience has increased exponentially. Research has shown that of 6.7 million Internet users, 8% of people were only willing to wait for two seconds for a page to load. After six seconds, one out of two people left or abandoned their shopping carts. [39]

And if the Internet usage on wait times reveals our lack of our ability to wait without restlessness, what other unimportant things dominate our sense of urgency?

The long checkout line at a store, traveling, waiting to get on the subway, or waiting in an airport are some examples. These are stressful because there is some level of uncertainty involved with the moment. There's a low-level anxiety or fear of being late, or the plane boarding and taking off on time.

Uncertainty breeds anxiety.

And anxiety is a meteor shower of "what-ifs."

The amount of time spent in any line is inconsequential throughout a lifespan, so it's not about the time. It's more about our mindset and attitude towards time and the situation. When there are timers letting us know the actual wait time, it lowers the level of anxiousness.

It isn't always about the ability to wait without becoming restless. It is also our capacity of doing so without agitation.

"The art of knowing is knowing what to ignore."

We have to understand what is unimportant. Most of life's setbacks and struggles are inconveniences, not tragedies. The short-term and our sense of urgency want us to operate on high alert, but this only leads to a lack of patience.

Urgency must proceed with caution toward any task that is unimportant. And if the most important thing is knowing what is important, perhaps the second most important thing is knowing what is unimportant.

The Origin of Species

Charles Darwin set sail on the ship HMS Beagle in 1831. It wasn't until 1835 that he visited the Galapagos Islands and began to formulate his theory of evolution. It wasn't until 1859, that he published the transformational book on evolution, *On The Origin of Species*. It took twenty-eight years of patience and persistence.

The Un-important

"Infinite patience produces immediate results."
— Wayne Dyer

We are all distracted by the unimportant. Both you and I suffer from it daily. We all struggle with waiting.

The unimportant is not bad. There are certain pleasures and simplicities in life that we enjoy, and these can be labeled unimportant.

The issue is that we cannot fuel these unimportant activities with any sense of urgency. Because when we do confound the unimportant with urgency, it spills into all areas of life.

We also cannot allow the unimportant to impact that which is important. We often feel like we can't slow down because we lost connection with the important. The more time we spend on trivial or unimportant niceties, it takes away from time and energy on the important.

— — —

The inability to wait without haste or restlessness started as infants.

Television used to be the time fillers for kids, but as technology improved, so did the dependence on modern day devices to pacify.

We placed iPads, or phones, in front of our kids at the restaurant, on the car ride *to* the restaurant, the dentist, on car ride *to* the dentist, etc. These tools actually promoted distraction and allowed the mind to wander. These electronic devices, like anything easy, became the norm and the regular. Basically, any situation that required an infant or toddler to wait without haste or restlessness was removed.

Kids no longer had to self-regulate their emotions; they merely got to watch a video. When this pattern was repeated over and over again for years, many kids did not develop the basic foundation to avoid becoming edgy, restless, or even fidgety.

The ball was pushed down the field as they got older and other gadgets and apps replaced being active or worse, being still.

Technology made waiting or being still very difficult, and almost made patience unnecessary. Why must we be patient when we can scroll?

Time tells us that it's never *too late,* however. We can strengthen our relationship with time and can learn how to be patient. And we can get there as fast as possible!

Visit Cantwaitbook.com

What's Your "Patience Personality?"

"The Fastest Way To Be Patient" Course

The Fastest Way To Get There

"Slow is smooth and smooth is fast."

This section is the fastest way to be patient. And if you, the reader, fast-forwarded to this section, then you are probably the person who needs patience the most.

The reading, relating, and applying patience in your own life is what makes an impact. It's not the information as much as it's the implementation that makes a difference.

— — —

Urgency trumps the important.

The take-home message is that we NEED to be urgent ONLY toward the important.

The important urgencies in life demand our focus, but even these require patience. We need to be patient in the moment and patient with the results.

Hostage negotiators realize time and patience are their greatest advantages in life and death situations.

Patience is vital when we encounter adversity, setbacks, or struggle. Adversity introduces us to our worst parts of ourselves and as a result, our default is that we act. We "do something" and our lack of forbearance and ability to pause, reflect, and think causes us more angst, stress, and feelings of being overwhelmed.

The skill of patience is most needed when things have gone astray. Patience is needed to navigate life.

The beauty is that every other mental skill hinges upon our relationship with time and our ability to be patient.

If you can wait, then you can win.

Improve your relationship with time

"I'll never be as great as I WANT to be. But, I am willing to spend my entire life trying to be as great as I CAN be."
— Kenny Aaronoff

The introduction of this book began with a focus on the power of time.

Time remains a powerful, uncontrollable constant. It's the same for everybody, whereas nothing else in life provides a level playing field. Those that desperately want control, stability, and peace in life need to look at their time.

When you improve the relationship with time, you'll also improve the relationship with yourself. Alas, a better relationship with time means improved patience.

Here are the fastest ways to be patient.

Focus on rhythm, not speed

Stress is a result of not being able to slow down. It's caused by too much time spent on the unimportant. Anxiety occurs when our mind is flooded with a meteor shower of "what-ifs." There's a better path instead of focusing on the speed from point A to point B.

Rhythm is quickness under control.

Life can hasten the tempo and cadence of how we operate and perform our best. Our circumstances can quickly change and both the test and the answer are to find your rhythm.

Slow is smooth and smooth is fast.

Routines help create rhythm and a proper cadence of life. There are natural routines that we do on the daily, from waking up, exercising, or brushing our teeth. Meetings, events, and even important decisions can have a rhythm to them and the most efficient ones have a familiar routine and structure.

However, we often aren't as sharp with our rhythm as needed. We are too focused on speed and not execution. Develop and enhance solid routines in many areas to assist with performance. For instance, our morning routine needs to be deliberate and focused. The first hour of the day sets the rudder for the rest. An evening routine to unwind and reflect, pause, breathe, plan, and express gratitude is sanctity.

And if you're not sure of your best rhythm, then start with slowing down.

Wealth

"No amount of money ever bought a second of time."

Money is a major cause of stress in the United States alone with 73% of Americans reporting finances and financial decision worry. [40]

A key to accumulating wealth is patience. As illustrated previously, the power of time is evident with money through the process of compounding. Earnings from both investment principal and accumulated earnings reveal the power of time. As senior financial broker, Michael Ball states, *"Time is the best diversification tool."*

Saving is a difficult skill to achieve because of the pull toward the urgent and immediate gratification. Saving money and earning 6% annually is not invigorating. A new car, boat, vacation, iPhone, outfit, or hosting the best wedding, or birthday party is exciting. Hence, the fastest way to be patient is to make saving and investing an unconscious, automated decision.

Everyone is a long-term investor until his or her stocks go down. Money, like anything else, encounters setbacks. Our money can't wait to be patient. Just remember as noted previously that the stock market has never lost money. But, as Morgan Housel, author of the book, *Psychology of Money* wrote, *"Progress happens too slowly to notice, but setbacks happen too quickly to ignore."*

The goal of every financial or news show is viewership. They know that the negative sells way more than the positive. As discussed earlier in the book, our mindset changes when we read negative reviews. Thus, turn them off and tune them out.

Wu Wei

It is the art and practice of doing without doing. This eastern philosophy is about strategic passivity. It's the complete opposite of the action bias and "don't just sit there, do something" mentality.

It's akin to the earlier sailboat analogy and making tiny adjustments along the way to our destination. Instead of doing nothing, it is about the natural unfolding of people and events by staying centered.

An example is focusing only on the process and not the outcome.

Instead of trying to will ourselves to make "it" happen, allow time to work in our favor. Allow that which is out of our control to unfold and play out before merely doing something.

"Don't just do something, sit there."

Flow is the goal

Immersion in the task at hand is always the best use of our time. "Flow" is an experience. It's achieved when we are fully engrossed in the moment. If you've been in that state, it can be magical.

Flow occurs more often with high challenge tasks because of the precision and skill needed. Surgeons, athletes, artists, programmers, writers, and runners all experience flow more frequently than the general population because of the inherent challenge coupled with their expertise.

The largest obstacle of flow is the starting and stopping of trivial actions. The task switching or context switching stems from replying to emails, calls, or commenting on LinkedIn, and taking five minutes here and there. These interruptions interfere with the major goal, which is total immersion into the task at hand. However, the more often we switch, the more it tasks our mental energy.

We can better achieve flow and being in the moment by starting small and allowing increments of time to let nothing bother you *(e.g. for the next thirty minutes, I will stay completely immersed in the activity at hand with no interruptions or distractions).*

Plan for flow

Flow happens naturally, we can't force it. However, we can put ourselves into situations that require our sole focus and attention.

The fastest way to be patient is to plan out your Monday the evening before, or plan the entire week ahead. There will be head winds and adjustments, but it will help keep the *main thing* the *main thing.*

We need to plan for times when we will be totally immersed into the daily activities at hand. This helps allow for our rhythm to unfold.

Ensure that the most important things are planned for. The unimportant and randomness of life will fill up the available time unless we plan for it.

And, when we have code reds pop up, with proper planning we can deal or delegate these time wasters.

When possible, plan well in advance for people, places, and things, such as vacations, parties, doctor appointments, zoom calls, kids' events, and so on. This will help ensure a calmer approach. When you schedule a vacation or upcoming challenge, it helps enhance our relationship with time. We plan around and anticipate it.

Change your perception

In order to appreciate the power of time, we must change our perception of time. We must experience time differently. Time is often something that just happens without much conscious thought. It's only when we are stressed or overwhelmed or behind, that we decry, *"I don't have enough time."*

Without proper perspective, any "waiting" that we do is considered equal in time, which is true. However, we don't perceive time as equal unless we are in touch with it.

Thus, one way to build perspective is to perform activities that make you hyperaware of the essence of time.

For instance, take one minute of a cold shower or plunge into an ice bath. Hop on an assault bike for one minute and ride as hard as possible. Do a row workout for five minutes to see how far you can go. Hold your breath for a minute. Close your eyes and without counting, see if you can guess when one minute is up.

These perspective activities are the same amount of time as waiting in line or being stuck in traffic.

Another way to improve your perspective and relationship with time is to connect with others. It automatically changes our perspective when we witness others who have overcome tough challenges and obstacles. It can also provide a sense of confidence because of the concept that *"if they can do it, so can I."*

Confidence is patience. When we connect with others, we can also see the roadmap that they took and the time commitment as well.

Change your perspective and your patience will grow.

Conduct a time audit

The goal of a time audit is to examine and record how you actually spend your 84,600 seconds per day.

It's sometimes painful because it illuminates where we can improve our relationship with time. However, it's an important exercise because it reveals how we truly spend or waste our time.

The goal is to bring what is important, your intentions, and your actual allocation of time into alignment.

Focus on experiences, not things

The brand new pair of shoes is nice. We love the smell and the look and the feel of them. In the beginning, we keep them extra clean, careful not to get any dirt on them.

But, this feeling eventually passes and they become like every other old pair of shoes. Some other "thing" needs to fill that void. You can substitute the shoes example for any other material object.

I'm not saying things aren't nice and aren't to be enjoyed, but that we too often neglect experiences.

Research shows experiences bring more happiness than stuff. Experiences are related to our time.

Everything is temporary, but experiences can be different. Trips, events, movies, and concerts provide a shareable connection. There's anticipation for the event and a post-recall that provides long-lasting memories. Even a poor experience can provide a good story to be shared later on.

Experiences not only connect us to others, but they also connect us to time. Each experience provides a specific time stamp to where we were in life during that moment. These connections with time get stronger the further away we get from it.

An experience provides us an opportunity to re-live those moments. Try this: Go back through your phone and share those special moments with the people involved. Watch how your perception changes.

Combat the threats to important urgencies

Coach Dick Vermeil won a Super Bowl with the St. Louis Rams in 1999. Upon taking the helm as head coach, he inserted a saying that embodied the identity of the team. He would often announce to the team, *"There's no easing into a street fight."*

It represented a mindset and identity that when it was time to practice and play, the team would be ready.

We need to know WHEN to be urgent and HOW to be patient. When we are urgent toward the important things and people in our lives, then we will be at our best.

Parkinson's Law illuminated the four specific threats to efficiencies and productivity. Stress and doubt can often arise because our company, team, or ourselves have not maximized our production.

Identify inefficiencies

The famous Sydney Opera House was to be completed in four years. It took over fourteen years. Its costs were 1000% over budget as well.

The bureaucracy that existed within the planning, development, and construction caused severe complications and major delays. Any sense of urgency to the project was eliminated.

Organizations seem to innately have a desire to expand, regardless of the tasks to be completed. As Parkinson noted, subordinates are hired not as competition, but more work is still created for everyone.

In general, meetings have been identified as causing major organizational inefficiencies. Hence, three causes of inefficient meetings are: 1) too frequent, 2) poorly timed, and 3) badly run. [41]

- Reduce meetings

  Leadership within organizations reported that meetings are a necessary evil. [41] Research has shown that leadership sees it as a way to foster a culture of collaboration. Therein lies the issue. Time is the most important resource and meetings cut deep into the time needed to achieve flow and significant progress. More "whitespace" in people's calendars means the potential exists for more progress.

- Have an assigned leader

  Part of the errors within the Uvalde catastrophe was that no one assumed real leadership. Diffusion of responsibility occurred which led to tragic time delays. It's easy to blur responsibility unless one is put in charge and held accountable.

- Protect the mission

  Inefficiencies will continue to exist unless clear and specific goals are created and followed through. The mission of the project and task must be protected. Teams and individuals that understand how their role fits within the larger mission are significantly more productive.

Remove excess time

The difference between a steak and a filet is cutting out the fat.

When you *allow* yourself a certain amount of time to devote to a project or task, you remove excess time and increase productivity.

Plan for and set aside specific blocks of time every day to accomplish certain tasks. For instance, the goal for writing my books was to write for one hour every day. Writing was also completed in the early morning when my attention and creativity were best.

The hardest tasks of the day also need to be whenever our energy is highest.

Personally, the morning time is blocked out and strictly devoted to writing and existing clients. The morning is when I'm able to tackle that which demands my utmost attention. Afternoons are not blocked out, because that is the time for the less important urgencies or code reds.

Law of triviality

"If everything is important, then nothing is." — Patrick Lencioni

When we know what is most important, then we can be urgent toward the important. The law of triviality will emerge unless we remain focused on the important things.

This strategy often requires a time audit and re-examining our priorities every year, month, week, and day.

Don't panic

Remember the life-threatening issue that panic caused scuba divers. We are thankfully above water, but the lesson is exactly the same.

When others are losing their head, you need to be able to keep yours. Regardless the cause of panic, the reaction is to do something, anything. And making rushed decisions is when we get into trouble that compounds upon itself. That's why mistakes occur in bunches. We hurry and rush instead of pausing and thinking.

Rest, reset, breathe, take a break, call a time-out, and/or remove yourself from the situation, but do not make a haste decision. It is uncomfortable not knowing exactly what to do. We all want assurances in life, and we will have to make tough decisions without knowing all of the range of outcomes.

Just don't panic! Stay focused with a clear mind.

If You Can Wait, You Can Win

"Genius is eternal patience."
— Michelangelo

S tress is not the issue.
In order for any muscle to grow, it must be stressed just past its current capabilities. Stress is necessary and the mind is no different.

The issue isn't that we **over-train** our mind, it's that we **under-recover**!

Patience is recovery of the mind.

Physical recovery for instance includes nutrition, hydration, stretching, and rest.

We can train and stress the body to handle higher demands, but if we don't properly recover, the gains we make will be limited and our risk of injury increased.

In order to improve mentally, we need to stress our mindset with goals, aspirations, achievements, etc. But we need to properly recover our mind as well.

If we don't recover with patience, then it undercuts all of the hard work that we've done.

No one can force you to recover or be patient. It has to come from an awareness of "*what my life will look like*" with improved patience.

There are four laws to the skill of patience: Acceptance of things and people, assurance for a better future, absence of resentment, ability to wait without haste or restlessness.

Twenty-Five Seasons

Dusty Baker won a World Series as a player in 1981. It took him twenty-five years of coaching before he would win his first as a manager. He went through five teams, twelve post-seasons, a stroke, and cancer before finally winning the championship. During the post-game, on the field interview, the first question asked was, "What's next?" The beloved Dusty Baker replied, " I want two."

Acceptance of things and people

This too shall pass

If things are going poorly, remember, *this too shall pass.*

If things are going great, unfortunately, *this too shall pass.*

We can't have it both ways.

The relationship with time must be rooted in acceptance. It is intended as a liberator of your circumstances. Time is the most precious resource and acceptance of this fact is freeing.

Robert Frost won the Pulitzer in 1924 for his poem, "Nothing Gold Can Stay." In it, he beautifully illuminates that nothing good in life can stay. Everything is temporary.

We must truly experience the good times and appreciate the joy. Celebrate, reflect, process, have a ceremony, etc. But, develop a routine and rhythm around success that allows you to enjoy it because this too shall pass. Be sure not to quickly rush to "next season" or what's next until processing the completion of a mountaintop moment.

Success is temporary, so the feelings after and surrounding such an event or accomplishment may leave one feeling empty.

Basketball Hall of Famer, Grant Hill, never displayed any basketball memorabilia in his home. Nothing would show that he was a professional basketball player. No trophies, magazine covers, nothing. He didn't want to "get soft" and wanted to always stay in the pursuit mode.

He regretted it.

He said, *"You have to celebrate when you do well to fully enjoy it."* Don't be so busy chasing it that you don't enjoy the successes along the way.

When we reach the mountaintop, we have to come back down. It's not so much about reaching it as it is going through the struggle to reach it. Hence, breathe, experience it, and allow yourself to enjoy it.

Because it is temporary, and yet, we have spent so much time chasing it, we think this accomplishment will fill the emptiness, or we'll find "the answer." It can be a major letdown because we return and find out we are *mostly* the same as before the accomplishment.

Thus, others will always notice the product, but the process is just as important.

Things don't go according to plan, they go according to our preparation

Johan Swanepoel has been a professional caddy since 2013. He has caddied most notably for his South African countryman, Christiaan Bezuidenhout.

During a practice round at the PGA Tour event in Las Vegas, he had Christiaan hit several shots into a specific par-3 hole. He jokingly announced, "You can't rush perfection."

Preparation is key.

Things will not always go according to plan. Screws fall out all of the time; the world is an imperfect place. What we can depend upon is our level of preparation to handle the adversity.

When our time is not utilized properly toward the important, then our preparation will suffer. And the preparation needs to include that we must accept people and situations as they are.

If we spend time trying to influence others and situations, it takes away from the focus needed on the important. This doesn't mean allowing whoever to do whatever they want. It means for us to stay focused and not get too caught up with controlling situations and people.

Assurance for a better future

Process > product

"The process takes perspective and the product takes patience."

Results are like the sun; it is nice, but we can't stare at it. If we are only focused on the product, the outcome, and the results, then our perspective will remain incorrect.

The perspective that is required is that *this too shall pass.* Your goal is to stay rooted inside of the process and connected with time.

As you're already aware, anything worth achieving will not only require "hard work and toil" but also patience.

No matter how bad or painful our circumstances, it only takes one moment, person, or decision to turn everything around. Hence, patience allows us to stay steadfast through the hardships, strife, and struggle along the path. Strangely enough, the harder the struggle and the more that we overcome, the deeper meaning it provides.

As Muhammad Ali stated, *"It's not the mountain to climb that wears you out, it's the pebble in your shoe."* The climb is so important that it's often the small things that bother us. We can allow inconveniences, stressors, and adversity to impact our overall wellbeing.

And when we do have breakthroughs, hinge moments, and successes, patience provides us inward peace, satisfaction, and fulfillment.

Patience is the skill that allows us to appreciate success, so we are not "onto the next" with such urgency. Perspective is difficult, because the product is always staring back at us demanding our attention.

Know your triggers

There's always an emotional trigger when we become stressed, anxious, or overwhelmed.

It happens to all of us. We can quickly lose hope because we're only focused on the product.

These triggers can occur at any time. It may be at night when we are tired, or because we have too many tasks to perform and haven't delegated. Perhaps we failed to prioritize the important over the urgent. It might occur when your golf group has fallen behind and someone wants to let them play through.

Usually, when triggered, emotions are involved and we are no longer in control. It's crucial to know your triggers and have a plan for how to handle them.

My three triggers unfortunately are often when driving, when technology fails, or I've lost something.

When we live in a state of hurry, it's a signal to reconnect with the power of time and re-establish a rhythm in the situation. Know the situations that can trigger you.

Nothing bothers you

The minor annoyances happen to all of us. The more frequent that the little things bother us, reveals that something more important is off.

Assurance for a better future means an attitude of confidence. It's the focus that *"I don't need everything to go my way in order for me to be successful in this moment."*

The solution is to make a commitment that for [this situation] "I'm not going to let anything bother me." "It doesn't matter what happens, I'll remain focused and patient." If it's a priority, then you can do it.

Watch how this small goal alone can build patience and confidence.

Technology frustrations, for instance, are common. It never seems that technology quits working at convenient times, either. Realize the power of time and that five weeks from now, this frustration won't matter if we respond correctly. So, have a goal to "let nothing bother you."

Finish strong

An emotional trigger is when there are too many unfinished projects. These unfinished tasks can weigh on your mind and use up prime mental real estate. Then all unfinished projects or tasks eventually become urgent. We can lose hope that we can be successful with too many loose ends.

Thus, whatever *it* is, finish strong.

When you complete a project, it frees up time and space. Don't save the last little bit for later, finish it now!

Start with the hardest project or drill or task and finish. If it's an ongoing long-term project, then set a time block and make sure you leave yourself in a good spot to pick it up later. Assurance stems from knowing that you can complete the hardest of tasks.

Absence of resentment

Vitamin "N"

"You've got to say 'no,' but when you say 'no,' that pisses people off." — Steve Jobs

When you say "no" to others, it frees up your time.

When you say "no" to different things, it allows you to say "yes" to the correct things. Saying "yes" sounds like being a team player, but it can steal your time.

Saying "no" is a time saver! It may be painful to do so, however, it is only a bruise, not a tattoo. As reiterated in this book, time is your most precious resource, thus you must protect it.

There's a default on which projects, meetings, or cups of coffee you can say "no." Ask yourself the question: *"does this have the potential to make an important relationship?"* If the answer is no, then consider the real reason for having the meeting.

The importance of saying "no" is so you do not develop resentments towards yourself. Choose disappointment over resentment.

I receive emails every week asking to meet and "pick my brain." I sometimes struggle with saying "no" as well, so I'll use time as an excuse.

Remember, time leads the scoreboard for excuses, so when you use it, people feel a need to accept it.

For instance, if saying "no" is a barrier in some situations, then use these alternatives:

- "I'm not sure how I would do that."
- "I'm sorry, but that just doesn't work for me."
- "I'm not sure I have time for that right now."
- "I appreciate the offer, but the timing isn't good right now."
- "I would consider it in the future, when I have more time."

As Warren Buffet also stated, *"The difference between successful people and really successful people is that really successful people say 'no' to almost everything."*

Respond, don't react

How do you respond when you're interrupted? Our reactions are usually incorrect because they are filled with emotion. When we react, we have temporarily succumbed to our emotions.

Unfortunately, a poor reaction to an important moment can require much cleanup and, worse, it can have tragic consequences. Too often, people develop resentments toward themselves or others after such events.

The path to patience is being able to respond, not react.

When we respond, it means that we have utilized time to our advantage. We have paused, taken a breath, and reset.

Responding means acceptance of the situation and noticing when we're triggered. When we respond, we stay ready to effectively handle situations and people.

Grief and grieving

Time does not always heal all wounds, but it can provide us perspective to our pain. If we do not transform our pain however, we will transmit it. We'll develop resentment around situations, others, and ourselves.

Grief is the overwhelming feeling of loss. It is the urgency of loss and the feeling arrives at various times. We may experience grief hundreds of times over months or years.

Grieving on the other hand is the process of allowing time to work. If we can sit with the pain, uncover it, and be patient, we can see the gift that time can provide. We will find that grieving is a universal feeling that connects us with others.

Ability to wait

Maximize the transitions in life

Remember, no matter what, we'll have to wait, so it matters how we behave while waiting. The question is: can wait without haste or restlessness?

Transitions can be major or minor in life. Minor transitions occur frequently such as traveling from one place to another.

There's a rhythm we establish during these sorts of transitions that can either help us or hinder us. If we only focus on speed, we're apt to show up rushed, stressed, or anxious. We become overwhelmed because we are not hitting the pause and reset button. When we maximize the transitions and establish a rhythm, we are more likely to arrive at our destination cool, calm, collected, and ready to go.

An NFL strength coach once shared about maximizing his transitions after a loss. He would show up at his house and literally repeat to himself and convince himself that "he won." He did it so his wife and kids would not be affected by a sour mood.

There are also major life transitions such as moving, becoming a parent, new job, new roles, and so on. These transitions simply require patience to establish a different rhythm of life.

We often miss so much when we are in a rush to get "there." We only recognize how much we miss after time reveals it.

To quote Ferris Bueller, *"Life moves pretty fast, if you don't slow down from time to time, you could miss it."* And another reveal of the speed of time is that the iconic movie was made in 1986.

Scroll past through your pictures from years ago and you'll be reminded of the power of time.

Slow down when transitioning in life from situation to situation. Be smooth in your approach. Be in the moment, especially during transitions.

Build margin in life

"Margin is the space between our load and our limits." — Dr. Richard Swenson

Living with little margin in life means there's often a sense of urgency toward everything. If we are in a rush all of the time, then we have little room for error or mistakes.

Sooner or later, this will catch up to us. A sign that increased margin is needed is when we feel overwhelmed. When we feel overwhelmed, it's often that we are doing too much. There's little emotional flexibility and it's death by a thousand duck bites.

If we can't wait without haste or restlessness then we need more margin.

Instead of working on specific mental skills to combat being stressed or overwhelmed, first examine your relationship with time. Increase the margin between what we can carry and what we "think" we can carry.

What occurs when we are stressed and overwhelmed is we are trying to do it all. These are instances when we need to delegate tasks and get assistance with building more margin in life.

Leave fifteen minutes earlier

Only a school bus can arrive *later* rather than *earlier*. If a school bus arrives early, no one is there and everyone is urgently running toward the bus stop.

Life is not like that; when you provide yourself margin for your travels, you make time your ally. Leaving early assures that you won't be as stressed or anxious getting to your destination.

Are you a person who is always hurried?

We've all made this mistake and the sheer panic or stress that can ensue from not allowing enough time is painful. One way we build more margin in life is to simply leave earlier.

This doesn't require discipline, either. It merely asks for you to have a better relationship with time.

Crush procrastination

Procrastination sadly serves a benefit. It comes at a cost, however. That cost is stress and the anxiety of waiting until the last minute. It's like junk food, because it'll fill us up in the short-term, but make us fat in the long-term.

Procrastination reflects our attitude towards time. However, again, patience is achieved first through a better relationship with time.

If someone in your family procrastinates, just note that this is just a symptom of a larger issue. Procrastination is linked with depression, lower self-esteem, and increased anxiety.

The way we combat the issue is to set time blocks and remove excess time. Shifting the issue away from behavior and merely changing the perception of time will increase productivity.

For example, once a time block is in place and, with patience, the attitude shifts from an "I have to" attitude to "I'm allowed to."

Removing excess time works to help us wait.

Pray for patience

"The fruit of the Spirit is love, joy, peace, patience, kindness, goodness, faithfulness, gentleness, self-control." —Galatians 5:22-23

It is hard to wait.

I need help. I need others in my life to help cultivate patience.

Paul The Apostle wrote in the book of Galatians that the fruits are gifts of the Holy Spirit to help us. One of the ways we access these gifts is to pray and ask to receive them.

And if that doesn't work, then pray again because God sometimes answers "ask me again tomorrow."

I don't believe that if we pray for patience, then God will put us in situations where we need to be patient. That is a clever saying, but the truth is that stress, anxiety, and being overwhelmed already exist. The path to patience may be to simply ask for help.

When we have patience it shows up in many ways.

Patient with ourselves.
Patient with other people.
Patient with results.
Patient with affliction.
Patient with situations.
Patient with development.
Patient with loss.
And patient with life.

Thank you for your patience

When we announce, "thank you for your patience," it provides a different energy than saying, "sorry I'm late."

A massive compliment is when we thank someone for his or her patience. Since many of us simply don't feel that we are patient, when we are recognized for it, it provides us with a special feeling.

It's similar to thanking someone for his or her time. When we thank them for their time, it's acknowledging the most precious resource that they have.

It provides us all with an emotional boost.

Visit Cantwaitbook.com

What's Your "Patience Personality?"

"The Fastest Way To Be Patient" Course

Continue the path of patience

"Every end is a new beginning."
— Marianne Williamson

You must be patient if you made it through the entire book. Thank you for reading.

To extend your own results and impact, here are some additional resources to help you and your team.

— — —

Books

If want to go at your own pace and still consume the information best suited for you, check out all of our books at drrobbell.com/books

Mental Toughness Podcast With Dr. Rob Bell

We interviews experts, coaches, and athletes about mental toughness and their Hinge moments. You'll get inspired and receive amazing strength, hope, and experience. Listen and subscribe on drrobbell.com/mental-toughness-podcast/

Keynote Speaking and Workshops

One of my favorite things is being able to spread the word and inspire, energize, and treat teams and organizations. Whether this is from the stage, boardroom, or locker room, being able to teach the mental game is our passion. You'll know the impact when your team performs its best when it matters THE MOST. Details at drrobbell.com/keynote-speaker

I Can't Wait To Be Patient Coaching

We've created and organized a successful course for you: *I Can't Wait To Be Patient.* If you're looking for the fastest way to get there, then visit us at caintwaitbook.com

One-on-One Coaching

A coach is someone who takes you where you want to go.

Our coaching is intensive and personalized for corporate athletes, elite, and professional athletes. If you *can't wait to be patient* and want to seize your Hinge moment and significance in life, schedule a call with us. Drrobbell.com

References

*"Patience is the number one attribute when
it comes to becoming a great chef."*
— Jason Atherton

1. Beutel, M. E., Klein, E. M., Aufenanger, S., Brähler, E., Dreier, M., Müller, K. W., Quiring, O., Reinecke, L., Schmutzer, G., Stark, B., & Wölfling, K. (2016). Procrastination, Distress and Life Satisfaction across the Age Range - A German Representative Community Study. *PloS one, 11*(2).

2. Wilson, T. D., Reinhard, D., Westgate, E., Gilbert, D., Ellerbeck, N., Hahn, C., Brown, C., & Shaked, A. (2014, July 4). *Just Think: The Challenges of the Disengaged Mind.* Science 345, 75.

3. Curtis, G. (2020, December 20). *Your Life In Numbers.* Dreams. https://www.dreams.co.uk/sleep-matters-club/your-life-in-numbers-infographic

4. Jena AB, Prasad V, Goldman DP, Romley J. (2015). Mortality and Treatment Patterns Among Patients Hospitalized With Acute Cardiovascular Conditions During Dates of National Cardiology Meetings. *JAMA Intern Med,* 175 (2) 237–244.

5. Ingvarsson, S., Augustsson, H., Hasson, H., Nilsen, P., von Thiele Schwarz, U., & von Knorring, M. (2020). Why do they do it? A grounded theory study of the use of low-value care among primary health care physicians. *Implementation Science: IS*, *15*(1), 93.

6. Cunningham SA, Mitchell K, Narayan KM, Yusuf S. (2008). Doctors' strikes and mortality: a review. Soc Sci Med. 67(11): 1784-8.

7. Siegel-Itzkovich J. (2000). Doctors' strike in Israel may be good for health. *BMJ (Clinical research ed.)*, *320*(7249), 1561.

8. Wolf, J. H., & Wolf, K. S. (2013). The Lake Wobegon effect: are all cancer patients above average? *The Milbank quarterly*, *91*(4), 690–728.

9. Tarrant C, Krockow EM (2022). Antibiotic overuse: managing uncertainty and mitigating against overtreatment. *BMJ Quality & Safety*, 31:163-167.

10. Clark, T., Johnson, A., & Stimpson, A. (2013, March). Going for three: Predicting the likelihood of field goal success with logistic regression. *7th Annual MIT Sloan Sports Analytics Conference.*

11. Zeelenberg, M., van den Bos, K., van Dijk, E., & Pieters, R. (2002). The inaction effect in the psychology of regret. *Journal of Personality and Social Psychology*, *82*(3), 314–327.

12. Dwyer, J., & Flynn, K. (2005, February 6). A September Morning. *The Washington Post.*

13. Man in Red Bandana (2017, September, 8). [Video]. IMDb. https://www.imdb.com/title/tt4687392.

14. Meng Zhu, Yang Yang, Christopher K Hsee, The Mere Urgency Effect, *Journal of Consumer Research*, Volume 45, Issue 3, October 2018,

15. Simpson, D., Bell, R.J. and Flippin, K.J., (2011). Caddying is Timing: An Interview with Joe Skovron, PGA Tour Caddy, *Journal of Excellence*, 14, 93-100.

16. Parkinson CN. *Parkinson's law: or, The pursuit of progress.* London: J. Murray; 1958.

17. Holiday Bonus: Impending Time Off Pushes the Pedal on Productivity (2015, December 15th). *New Jersey Business Magazine.*

18. Aronson, E., & Landy, D. (1967). Further steps beyond Parkinson's Law: A replication and extension of the excess time effect. *Journal of Experimental Social Psychology, 3*(3), 274–285.

19. Höcker A, Engberding M, Nieroba S, Rist F. (2011). Restriction of working time as a method in the treatment of procrastination. *Verhaltenstherapie.* 21 (4): 255–61.

20. Descamps, A., Massoni, S., & Page, L. (2016). Knowing When to Stop and Make a Choice, an Experiment on Optimal Sequential Sampling. *Behavioral & Experimental Economics eJournal.*

21. *Decision making in the age of urgency.* (2019). McKinsey & Company. https://www.mckinsey.com/capabilities/people-and-organizational-performance/our-insights/decision-making-in-the-age-of-urgency#/

22. Colvard, D & Colvard, L. (2003). A Study of Panic in Recreational Scuba Divers. *Undersea Journal.*

23. Stengle, J. (2022, July 19). *TIMELINE: Texas elementary school shooting, minute by minute.* AP NEWS. https://apnews.com/article/shootings-texas-education-school-6e37217b70e4977d985a1d1b50cc29fc

24. *The Myers & Briggs Foundation - MBTI® Basics.* (n.d.). 2003-2023, the Myers and Briggs Foundation. https://www.myersbriggs.org/my-mbti-personality-type/mbti-basics/

25. Akhtar, Salman (Feb, 2015). Patience. *Psychoanalytic Review,* 102 (1) 93-122.

26. How 22-Year-Old George Washington Inadvertently Sparked a World War. (2020, January 21). *History.com.* https://www.history.com/news/george-washington-french-indian-war-jumonville

27. DiMeglio, S. (2022, March 21). *Justin Thomas will continue to call on patience as he comes close again at Valspar Championship.* Golfweek.

28. Ingraham, C. (2016b, June 23). *When you will most likely hit your creative peak, according to science.* Washington Post.

29. Liu, L., Wang, Y., Sinatra, R., Giles, C. L., Song, C., & Wang, D. (2018). Hot streaks in artistic, cultural, and scientific careers. *Nature, 559*(7714), 396–399.

30. Staff, H. (2022, August 25). More than half of millennials expect to be millionaires - *Hella Wealth.*

31. Heck PR, Simons DJ, Chabris CF. 65% of Americans believe they are above average in intelligence: Results of two nationally representative surveys. *PLOS One.* 2018 Jul 3;13(7).

32. Svenson, O. (1981). Are we all less risky and more skillful than our fellow drivers? *Acta Psychologica, 47*, 143-48.

33. Zuckerman, E. W., & Jost, J. T. (2001). What Makes You Think You're So Popular? Self Evaluation Maintenance and the Subjective Side of the "Friendship Paradox". *Social Psychology Quarterly, 64*(3), 207-223.

34. Singh, R. S. (2020). Overconfidence. *New England Journal of Entrepreneurship, 23*(1), 25–39.

35. Gabay, R., Hameiri, B., Rubel-Lifschitz, T., & Nadler, A. (2020). The tendency for interpersonal victimhood: The personality construct and its consequences. *Personality and Individual Differences, 165*, 110134.v

36. StudyFinds.org. (2022, April 16). *Survey: 1 in 4 adults checks phone less than a minute after waking up.* Study Finds

37. M. A. Killingsworth, D. T. Gilbert. (2010). A wandering mind is an unhappy mind. *Science* 330, 932.

38. Gervis, Z. (2019, May 22). *Top 10 tech stresses that frustrate Americans.* New York Post.

39. *How technology is ruining our patience – The Stute.* (2020, November 19).

40. American Psychological Association. (2015). Stress in America: Paying with our health.

41. Perlow, L. A. (2017, June 26). *Stop the Meeting Madness.* Harvard Business Review.

Made in the USA
Monee, IL
15 August 2023

41008441R00105